B R A N D Y W I N E

Elizabeth Humphrey

Michael Kenna

12/14/90

BRANDYWINE

ELIZABETH HUMPHREY

PHOTOGRAPHY BY
MICHAEL KAHN

The **Jared** *Company*

WILMINGTON, DELAWARE

Front Cover: Hibernia in summer

Author: Elizabeth Humphrey
Photographs: Michael Kahn
Editor: Larry Elveru
Foreword: James H. Duff
Map: Scott Boettger
Design: Michael Brugman
Publisher: Alisa J. Dadone

The Jared Company
833 Locust Street
P.O. Box 1948
Wilmington, Delaware 19899

Published 1990
Printed in Hong Kong
Library of Congress Catalog Card Number 90-5165
ISBN 0-89802-564-8
First Edition: October 1990

DEDICATION

Michael and I would like to dedicate this book to all who have worked to preserve and protect the Brandywine Valley.

ACKNOWLEDGEMENT

We would like to thank many people. Rick Davis, who loaned Michael his darkroom for endless hours. Our family and friends. And the administrators of many groups. Among them: The Brandywine Conservancy and River Museum; The Brandywine Valley Association; The Chester County Parks and Recreation Department, Department of Water Resources, and Agricultural Services; The Chester County Historical Society; Forward Lands; The Hagley Museum and Library; The New Castle County Water Authority; Wilmington Waterways, Inc., The Wilmington Department of Public Works; and The Winterthur Museum & Gardens.

To us, these groups are important not only for providing information or encouragement toward this book. We thank them for their interest in the Brandywine, and their desire that it remain a vital river.

C O N T E N T S

F O R E W O R D

"Certain mental pictures rise before the collector of memories at the simple mention, written or spoken, of the places he has loved." So said Henry James, whose elaborate pictures appear in his essays about many treasured places. The urge to depict and immortalize a place rises in some out of sheer love for it. So it must be with the book you now hold.

Elizabeth Humphrey and Michael Kahn both live along the Brandywine River and are devoted to their subject. They have skied and hiked beside it, canoed and swum in it, and studied it from end to end. They bring their best talents to it; the fine writing of one complements the carefully arranged visual images of the other.

No stranger to many in this region, Elizabeth Humphrey writes on a variety of subjects for many publications. She studied writing, among other places, at Harvard and in London, England. For a time she was a program assistant at the Yellow Springs Institute working with artists, scholars and their publications. This personal progress contributes to both her fine prose style and diligent research.

Photographs of the quality of Michael Kahn's develop from years of study, dedication and effort. He has held his own camera since age thirteen and is largely self-taught. He is an avid outdoorsman whose sympathies are visible in his photographs. For all but a few of the photographs reproduced here, he used a 4x5 inch view camera and a single lens.

Elizabeth has a technical advantage in presenting her work: her prose is complete before us. Michael's work, like all fine photography, cannot be reproduced well enough on a book's pages to convey the contrasts and surface qualities of the prints he makes by hand. Nonetheless, we learn from both their efforts, and we can always hope to see exhibitions of the original photographs.

The Brandywine Valley is a singular place that has long commanded attention and deserves it. Because of its importance, it has been served by books before, foremost among them *The Brandywine* by Henry Seidel Canby, part of the Rivers of America series in 1941. But no other book lets us visit such a diverse story on each page as does this present one, and no other book tells us so much about the contemporary Brandywine while exhibiting scenes we can find today.

From trickle to terminus is the course of this presentation. It allows lively pursuits, jumping backward and forward in history as this part and then that part of the Valley suggests a brief anecdote or a complicated story. The method is refreshing. Newcomers will learn much from it. Those who know the River will be fascinated by fresh discoveries. All will delight in these special pictures of a much loved place.

James H. Duff
Chadds Ford
January 1990

Note: Mr. Duff is the executive director of the Brandywine Conservancy, which works to preserve, protect, interpret, utilize, and display American artistic, natural, and historical resources, principally of the Brandywine region.

H E A D W A T E R S

As Welsh Mountain crosses from Lancaster into Chester County, it crests at 1100 feet above sea level and drops quickly to the gentler slopes that cultivate the Brandywine headwaters. The valley below has never known battle or tragedy, and it hasn't given in much to industry—or progress for that matter. It is a valley of rolling soil, plowed by mule teams and draft horses. The hills are veined by fledgling river branches, the skyline dotted with white barns, windmills, and towering silos. Houses here are simple, many dim at night with the glow of kerosene lanterns. And so the river land begins, as gentle and plain as the people who farm its banks.

Al Given believes the Brandywine is born on his property. "Yep, this is it. This is where it starts," he says, pushing his hoe through a clear trickle on the wooded slope of Welsh Mountain.

Al's cup hangs in a tree so that he can hold it to the spouting water that stays cool in midsummer, water that is pure and sweet as it leaves the rock. A ruined foundation, once home to the people who rimmed the spring with quarried stone, tumbles beside the dark hole. Al is the self-appointed caretaker of this first trickle that will join others to form the east branch Brandywine. He carries his hoe up the hill beside the cow pasture, along a wooded path, to rake the oak leaves from the narrow stream bed.

"I love it here. Nobody bothers ya," Al says. Yet the solitude of the stream is deceiving. Noise from the sandstone quarry on the ridge, a disc harrow grinding through rocks in a field below, dogs barking in an Amishman's kennel, and the squawk of turkeys in the barn to the south synchronize a rural cacophony.

The path descends steadily from the forest clearing toward the grove of pines that tower above the old man's house. To the left, a corn field awaits planting, and cows to the right rejoice at the tender green shoots that have filled their pasture. Al looks out across the valley. "I was born and raised here," he says. "I thought I may as well come back here and die."

Albert Given is seventy years old, retired from farming the land in the shadow of the mountain. He now plants fruit trees and blackberry bushes, hoes a small garden near the fields where he once drove a tractor up the rows, and piles corn beside his shed to attract the white-tailed buck that will provide sport and venison come hunting season.

The "coming back" involved a move of less than a mile. It seems he felt uprooted when his father sold the family farm in the valley and moved down the road apiece to the village of Suplee. When Al brought his family to the small house that looks down toward the farm where he had once risen with the dawn to do chores, it was a homecoming.

There is no river in this valley. Only a man-made lake and a spotting of small ponds where farmers' sons gather in summer to swim away the heat of farm chores. The headwater streams are like tender sprouts—the fledgling trickles that drain from the mountain seem to have barely the momentum to swell to a river's proportions. Yet there is a quiet energy in their flow. Sweetened by a run through the sandstone ridge, streams nourish crisp stalks of skunk cabbage and fern. The clear brooks cut into planted fields and widen as they take on feeder streams.

Al Given beside the source

To the south of the mountain, Struble Lake spreads plainly across a low basin. In the winter, it looks like a field snowed over, the ice fishermen dipping lines into icy groundhog holes and reeling up bluegill. In spring, it is choppy with wind. In summer, calm with the subtle paddle of canoers. And at the close of the year, when the neighboring fields have been harvested and the world turns brown, the water, too, becomes dark beneath the chill.

The main town, called Honey Brook, grew of a crossroads to support the vast farmland that surrounds it. Before the land was cleared for farming, and the hills sutured by paved roads, the wilderness beyond was a frightening thing. Three hundred years ago great chestnuts, white oaks, hickory and tulip poplars formed a dark canopy. The woods were a necessary track between towns, and Honey Brook once swarmed with stories brought by drovers to the crossroads inn. Tales of those who never returned from the forest and of bandits hiding in dense thicket danced in the minds of the townspeople.

Trucks now barrel up Routes 322 and 10 *en route* to a landfill and the factories to the north. The factory in town makes molasses, and huge grain elevators lift the local feed to storage tanks. Honey Brook Borough is a busy town, quieted by its outskirts of corn stalks, grass and wheat. Folks call both borough and the surrounding township Honey Brook, but it's clear which they're talking about by context.

Local lore and history are strong, for the simple woods and field that give water to the Brandywine offered hushed retreat even before the founding of the New World. Since then, groups of people not in step with the world around them, though closely attuned to their own faiths and culture, have settled here for centuries.

Where houses now fade into nightfall, a peaceable Indian tribe once tracked dark forests. The Lenni-Lenape were the first peace lovers in the valley, the original followers of a Great Spirit. Faith would later guide the Quaker brethren here, gone from the British Isles to find a place where life might be simple once again. To the Welsh and Scotch-Irish, the Brandywine headwaters grew from hills by which to remember their homelands as they continued to raise sheep in a new land. The Germans would settle in the valley, too, and finally the descendants of a radical Swiss religious sect—the Mennonites and Amish.

A few of the descendants of those earliest settlers remain here, but the most recent immigrants prevail. The Amish live today much as their forefathers did when their staid doctrine was written nearly 300 years ago. Simplicity has draped the headwater region like a crisp

Skunk cabbage

Mennonite children

white bonnet, and the presence of the quiet people is so strong and so fitting that it is difficult to believe that they are relative newcomers to the land.

Faith. Humility. Dedication. Servitude. For those they remain humble in the face of financial success. They believe God has called them to such a life, and ordained their connection to the land. It is said that the Amish, with their homespun equipment, are among the few who can turn a living from the soil. The plows that cut rows for alfalfa, corn, tobacco, and grains are considered antique. They wear out and they are repaired, year after year. The farmers' techniques, too, are old—and yet the fields sprout the best produce in the East.

Voltaire once said, "Nothing human is alien to me." Yet to the outer world there is a fascination about the gentle people. They refrain from the use of electricity. Amongst themselves, they speak a Germanic dialect, called Deitsch or Pennsylvania Dutch. They dress "plain"—the men in black pants and hat, the women in deep purple dresses and discreet aprons—and they drive to the market in somber buggies, closed dark and tight in the heat of summer. In neighboring Lancaster County, a day doesn't pass when the Amish families are spared the passing of chartered busses filled with tourists with their cameras and stares. Their towns are laden with giftshops and restaurants offering supposed Amish fare—towns called Bird-In-Hand, Intercourse, and the village they once named Paradise.

But life is a little quieter in Honey Brook. It's as though the tourist industry hasn't had time to catch on.

The Amish and the Mennonites sought solitude on the fertile land west of Welsh Mountain, drawn to Pennsylvania by William Penn's offer of a chance to flee persecution in Europe. The Quaker leader's mother was of Deutsch descent, he had travelled in the German principalities, and was sympathetic to those who had long struggled for religious freedom. Their forefathers had retreated from Zurich to purity in the Swiss Alps. Menno Simons, a reformed Catholic priest from Holland, and a conservative bishop named Jacob Amman, both felt life in sixteenth-century Europe had become wanton and frivolous. But perhaps Amman thought the world a little more rough than his fellow clergy did. The Amish leader eschewed progress in directing his people toward the simplicity of faith that the Bible passages told of the early Christian Church.

Amish barns and plow

The Amish remain more cautious of technology and involvement with the larger world than the car-driving, electricity-tapping Mennonites. Yet it's difficult to generalize about the two faiths. They are similar in doctrine but cleft over practice, forming more divisions amongst divisions than there are Amish and Mennonite surnames.

The lands first opened to them in this New World of civil and religious liberty, this rare place devoid of a state church, were to the north of Welsh Mountain. They moved from Philadelphia, through Germantown, toward Berks, Lebanon, and Lehigh, then to Lancaster County, which remains today the Amish stronghold. The shift eastward toward these Brandywine springs began with John P. Stoltzfus, who bought a big farm and mansion near the Suplee Railroad junction at the base of the mountain, while soldiers went off to fight the first world war. Growing Lancaster County Amish families moved east as the descendants of the pioneers who had settled along the Brandywine's feeder streams were beckoned from the soil by concrete towns and cities.

Most mail boxes along the roads in Honey Brook township read "Stoltzfus." And they are used frequently, for the Amish install telephones only for business and emergencies—and they do that with reluctance. When Don Piersol took on the job of Honey Brook postmaster in 1971, a slew of letters addressed to this Stoltzfus or that ran through his post office. As the numbers grew, he found a system to tell Jacob B. from Jacob K. and the Jonas on White School Road from the Jonas on Route 10.

"They use their initials," he said, "and the four carriers just know the families after a while." There are close to two hundred Amish families in Piersol's postal domain and, system or no system, sorting the Kauffmans, Glicks, Reihls, Kings and Fishers who move to the rural routes each year will remain a challenge.

The farms are vast, the roadway between houses distant, but the Amish feel the pinch of development. Even the Old Order makes some concessions in light of technology. They push on with their diesel engines, propane gas and compressed air to power tools and milking machines. They'll hire a driver to take them where their horses can't.

And while the gasoline costs that sink other farmers are absent from the Amishman's budget, the demand for corn and hay to fuel their hefty horses is a drain. The large families appear to the roadside

Round bale

observer nearly self-sufficient, but they share the burdens of other farmers. Their land is precious and exhaustible; vast acres are needed to produce enough crop to turn a profit. The scarcity of soil and the high cost of the little that is available forces the Amish families to divide property. Talk is intense when word of a local farmer considering sale to a developer leaks out.

Welsh Mountain is a barrier to development from the north, strained with the holding back. The fields just over the mountain ridge, off an exit from the Pennsylvania Turnpike, are scattered now with lines of houses painted pale shades. Factory outlet stores, highways, and industrial parks have sprung from the land like cardboard houses in a child's pop-up book. Roads tunnel through and around the mountain, and soon, people fear, the bulldozers may descend on Honey Brook to tear cornstalks from the soil.

People still call the clustered farms just east of town the LeBoutillier Tract. The French name seems misplaced on the spartan horizon, for the ten Amish farms there—each with a barn and silo, a carriage shed, and a five-bedroom house—are monuments to struggle and partnership.

Nearly a thousand acres cut by the West Branch of the Brandywine were up for sale in 1977 and developers circled over the open fields like buzzards. The carrion property might yield a suburban landscape, prepared on land that had been dormant for half a century. The people of Honey Brook township tried to prohibit a sale, and the owner of the land took the township to court. Then, as the taxpayers began to wonder if the struggle was worth the mounting court fees, a credit officer and a partnership of Amish farmers saved the land.

Russell Albright, loan officer for the local Farm Credit Service, knew that several of the farmers had sons of marrying age. And that, with the scarcity of land, those sons would be forced to work neighboring farms or turn to industry to support their families. He also knew that the land and the meandering branches of the Brandywine were vulnerable to a colorful plot plan. Using Albright's calculations, some farmers made an offer to buy the entire parcel, but the LeBoutelliers balked again.

More Amish farmers joined the ranks, the talk spun from offers to rejections to re-offers, and after two years, on the edge of defeat, ten Amishmen pulled themselves around a kitchen table at a dairy farm with a plan. Each of the farmers wrote on a piece of paper the highest price per acre he was willing to pay for the property. The secret ballots were collected, offers averaged, and they went to the township planning commission with an offer. The owners agreed to sell the parcel, and the Amishmen sat around the table again. This time to subdivide.

They sketched in their ten farms, each taking fields around the wooded, untillable slopes. A harmonious division, a process that Albright had seen take two years to complete, was accomplished in an evening. In the summer of 1980, the barn-raisings began.

Not all earn a living from the soil. At first you don't hear the hens in Melinda Stoltzfus' barn. Step just inside the adjoining room where she sorts and stacks the fresh-laid eggs and the clucking grows constant and raucous. The modest roost cages four thousand chickens, enough squawking hens to push out 116 dozen eggs each morning. The Stoltzfus sisters gather the eggs by hand and gently stack them in great wire baskets—brown, white, large and extra large. Some go to market, others await those who drive their cars or their buggies to the farm, enticed by a sign before the tidy white house along Pleasant View Road. Eggs for Sale. Theirs is a cottage industry.

Like many of their neighbors, the unmarried sisters draw income from the sale of produce and craft. Hand painted signs at the end of farm drives advertise the small enterprise in the countryside. Shoe repair, gladiolas, furniture repair and upholstery, leather, vegetables and quilts.

In a shop beside the Stoltzfus' egg room, the components of chairs—seats, legs, rungs and back slats—cut from black walnut, are neatly stacked. From their father, the sisters learned to make chairs, to soak and clamp and bend the wooden backs, and to operate the hydraulic lathe, drill, and sander powered by a diesel engine. There is no sign, the sisters don't advertise, and the furniture business has no name, and yet they are behind in filling orders for the chairs. The caning takes half a day in itself, longer for the oversized rockers made wide and sturdy to soothe tired bones.

It is the nose that first delights in Jonas Stoltzfus' harness shop, a mile or so away from the sisters' farm. The smell of rich, oiled leather is full and pungent as autumn rain on leaves. Then the eyes adjust to the dim rooms. The black, thick tannings grow brighter. Heavy studs, a vat of dark oil, piles of dusty, cracked collars awaiting rejuvenation for spring plowing line the shelves.

Eggs, the Stolzfus sisters' farm

Jonas' harness shop

Amish schoolhouse

When he was a farmer, harness making and repair were necessary chores. Jonas and his sons worked in a small cabin on the farmyard during the seventies, mending their own leather. His son now farms the fields and lives with his young family in the big white house where his father raised him. With the wedding, Jonas had built himself a small brick house so the new family would have room to grow. It's not uncommon, building an addition for the patriarch or a tidy new cottage beside the family home. The Amish have a name for it, *Grossdawdi* House.

Daniel Kauffman, too, has passed on his 80-acre farm to his son. Together they live on the property bordered by the narrow West Branch of the Brandywine and the quiet passing of Park Road as it descends from Honey Brook toward the Baron Hills. His beard is long and gray; he no longer works the thick earth.

While his son Amos hitches a team of six mules, Daniel repairs shoes. Some on the rack just inside his shop are patched upon patches. The air compressor chugs a heavy tune while he buffs and polishes. His equipment is old, his sewing machine a bulbous black Singer with foot pump treadle.

Kauffman's family moved east out of Lancaster when he was fourteen years old, and he began farming. There were few Amish families in Honey Brook then. Daniel Kauffman views the world clearly from his quiet farm. While moving about his shoe shop, he doesn't speak of "us" and "them," or condemn progress as though removed from its snare. He speaks of a different "walk of life" perhaps.

"The Amish have larger families and buy more farmland," he says. Their reason for forming a partnership like that on the LeBoutellier tract is that "they want the land. Nothing else." As a farmer, he said he shared the burden for the threat to the creek. Along with real estate developers and the landfill that abuts the West Branch source, he and the others do threaten the downstream Brandywine with their run-off from eroded fields and their fertilizers, both organic and chemical, that travel south with the water.

Kauffman spoke of the one-room schools his community has built. There are three, scattered between the farms. From its wooden porch to its tiny belfry, Pleasant View School looks like the one-roomers built two hundred years ago by early settlers. But the walls beneath the tan stucco are of cinder block. They were raised by a gathering of

Amishmen less than thirty years ago.

Seven boys sit beneath the swaying willow branches, eating sandwiches while their teacher talks with the girls just inside the heavy wooden door. The building is cozy and, in contrast to the childrens' unadorned homes, is decorated from floor to ceiling with colorful drawings. State names and their capitals were chalked neatly across the blackboard.

Mary Stoltzfus is eighteen years old. She never studied education, never went to school beyond the eighth grade, but she teaches twenty-five children in the single room of the oldest of the three schools. She teaches her students to add, subtract, multiply and divide; to identify states and countries on a map; to write and draw; and she teaches them to read. The Honey Brook librarian says that if the Amish children didn't sign books out as often as they do, the collection for young readers wouldn't circulate at all.

The Amish chose to separate their children not only to shield them from the public schools' secular ways, but to save money. Amish residents pay taxes to the local school district, and they support their own tiny schools without government assistance. "It costs less for us to have our own schools. The charge for each student in the public schools is so high," Kauffman says, "that taxes would be higher if our children attended."

When the one-room schools in the rural region grew to become a district, requirements had changed. Reading, writing, and arithmetic were overshadowed by a more elaborate curriculum, including athletics, which the Amish consider worldly. Farm work and carpentry, a truer education for their lives, was not rewarded. Worse yet, attendance at the public schools was compulsory until age sixteen. Fathers needed their boys in the field.

Football coaches, advanced trigonometry and the senior class musical would not serve an Amish student well. The United States Supreme Court agreed in a landmark 7-0 ruling on May 15, 1972, that exempted the Amish and Old Order Mennonites from compulsory attendance laws beyond the eighth grade.

"It is neither fair nor correct to suggest that the Amish are opposed to education beyond the eighth-grade level," Chief Justice Warren Burger wrote. "What this record shows is that they are opposed to conventional formal education of the type provided by a certified high

Amish farm, Honey Brook

18

school because it comes at the child's crucial adolescent period of religious development." And it was set in law.

Just beyond the Kauffman farm, two young boys prepared teams to plow long rows over the gentle hills beside their farm. They worked quickly; the sky was gray with rain that would soon fall. One hitched four draught horses—two grays, a bay and palomino—to the plow and gently slapped the reins across their massive rumps. As the animals pulled the harrow through the coarse March mud, their sweat rose through the air as steam. It was as if they were burning.

Occasionally, with their quiet plows, the Amish farmers turn up arrowheads. How distant is their faith from that of the red men that once planted corn in these fields? Perhaps they worship a different God, yet, like the Indians, they revere nature as a gift and consider it a privilege to diligently gather its bounty.

As a farmer rubs the sweat from his team in the barn, and the fresh-cut rows of earth begin to dry to a lighter dust across the fields, Calvin Smoker parks his car beside the road and begins to walk the furrows. He eyes the freshly tilled earth like a beachcomber scanning sand at low tide. His Saturday morning search for Indian relics may perplex the farmers; it is a hobby—a pleasure "to go out and find them, clean them up and display them."

Smoker has just returned from one of his fifty favorite sites, kept secret because arrowhead hunting gets a little competitive, where he scavenged a broken banner stone amongst the toss of dirt and rock. It has made his day. He says he can't imagine the shaped and polished rock had been used just to weight a spear. "It's too ornate for that from what I can see," he says. "Like sculpture."

"I found just a half. If you find a whole one, well, you take your wife out to dinner," he said. In 1955, when Smoker married his wife Mabel, they moved into a new house and started a small vegetable garden. While digging they began to find arrowheads. Then they began walking out to inspect freshly tilled fields with eyes to the ground, and a passion was born. Three thousand artifacts and thirty years later, boxes of cataloged relics await the day when he can arrange them in a museum beneath the garage of his house in the woods.

Some of the rocks are obvious artifacts, a chunk of bowl that was carved from soapstone, primitive drill bits, scrapers to clean hide, and quartz arrowheads as clear as bottle glass. "You walk slow and examine a lot of stones," he says. "Sometimes I'll see a little piece, and it won't look like much until I actually dig it out of the ground. Other people would walk right by something like that."

Smoker's tool is a fishing rod he picked up at a yard sale. "I go out and find these things and I think, 'Hey—I'm the first person who picked that up since an Indian held it in his hand.'"

The red men burned timber through the forests to clear cover, crafting knives, tomahawks, spears, clubs, and bows to hunt game. They carried home the kill and removed the meat carefully, the old women cleaning and drying hide to make leggings and skirts, and warm beds for earthen wigwam floors. The men pieced together canoes to ride the Brandywine and gather fish, planted maize, beans, pumpkins, and tobacco, and gathered wild fruits.

The Lenni-Lenape first built their encampments at the base of the mountains, following the clear waters of the West Branch Brandywine to a place now called the Baron Hills. They fished the northern waters of the *walachneu*, the sweet stream. Their belief in the Great Spirit guided them through the forests and formed the basis for their society.

The white settlers called the red men the "Delawares." In 1682, the year after King Charles II granted the pacifist son of a prominent English admiral the land that would become Pennsylvania, the Indians saw white men. It wasn't long after William Penn's fellow Quakers had sailed from England to the shores of the Delaware to form a new settlement, Philadelphia, that the settlers ventured west to slowly clear the trees and acquire the land. Some of the Indians who lived beside the headwaters had heard of, perhaps even seen, the Swedes, Finns, and Dutch who had landed fifty years earlier at the mouth of the Brandywine many miles to the south. Yet the Quakers weren't like the northern Europeans. Rigid discipline bound the Society of Friends to plain living. Their aim was to achieve "the simplicity which keeps the soul open to the inner light"—to live as Christ taught by practicing simplicity, equality, and peace.

"Justice Bennet of Derby was the first to call us Quakers," wrote their leader, George Fox, "because I bid them tremble at the word of the Lord. This was in the year 1650." Like the Amish, the Friends had no need for ritual, for sacraments, or an ordained clergy. And again like the Amish, living according to the rules of a stringent spiritual code was undoubtedly difficult. The Friends challenged the established

Page 21: Windmill

20

social traditions, and for that they had been chastised in England. Oliver Cromwell said, "I see there is a people risen, that I cannot win either with gifts, honours, offices, or places, but all other sects and people I can."

There was a singular harmony about the lives of individuals, families, and communities of Quakers in a distant and barren land. Friends' meeting houses still draw worshipers throughout this valley, many descendants of the early settlers. Quakers who continue to value simplicity and through the years have revered education and the rewards of a work ethic, while eschewing violence and social injustice.

Penn's woods were dense with oak, poplar, maple and birch when his Quaker brethren first moved west across the Great Valley from Philadelphia. It could be said that King Charles II set the first deed restriction here. For every five acres of land cleared, he mandated that one of woods was to be left. On those acres that the settlers cleared, there remained charred stumps of trees, and after the fashion of the Indians they planted corn. Chester County was one of Penn's three original counties, and, though then a wilderness of scattered Indian villages, he and his followers respected its first inhabitants. Having heard them speak, he called their tongue "in signification full, like shorthand in writing."

"I must say, that I know not a language spoken in Europe," Penn wrote, "that hath words of more sweetness or greatness, in Accent and Emphasis, than theirs."

As the Quakers had fled from intolerance in the British Isles in hopes of creating a better place, they befriended the natives by conviction. Penn knew the land belonged to them. He paid the Lenni-Lenape, "the Original People," with flints, needles, sugar, molasses, and pipes. And, as the Quakers had hoped, the Indians lived peaceably with the white settlers—without the raids and massacres so common in New England settlements and others to the south.

But the Lenapes' peaceful solitude, which had been interrupted only by raids of the fish-hoarding Susquehannas from the west, would soon end. There would be other settlers to the land below Welsh Mountain, people who were unlike the plain sects to the north or the Quakers who first plowed these fields. People who felt superior to the Indians, cheated and robbed them. And even the well-meaning amongst the light-skinned men, some of them Quakers, would dam their precious creeks to draw power for manufacture. Unfamiliar with the Indians' seasonal migrations, they might take land presumed deserted. The Lenape would return to see their ancestral villages planted with the white man's crops, claimed by his homes and barns.

Allummeuchtummen, according to a German Moravian who learned and translated the Lenape tongue 250 years ago, means "go away weeping." The Indians went west, leaving behind only legend and the bits of discarded tools that resurface in the soil that lines the banks from the river's source to tide.

Enriched by forests south and east of Honey Brook, the Brandywine leaves the gentle limestone valley. The East and West Branch begin to ask for attention; small bridges span the banks grown too wide now to push as they had through culverts beneath the road. The growing creeks test their currents and chisel deeper into the earth. The Brandywine will soon come of age.

EAST BRANCH

Every so often along its descent, the East Branch of the Brandywine will take sustenance from a tiny spring. And with each new feeder, it swells just a little bit wider until eventually you can actually hear the water pushing southward through its stony trough. That sound, the sonance of swelling water, once meant power as towns were settled alongside the creek, across this valley. Rushing water was channeled through races and over dams to supply power to the furnace master, to the millers of grist and lumber, and to the paper makers.

Wood was also the catalyst to that power. Board formed the slats of the water wheel and built bridges. Logs framed the first houses and the eaves atop mills beside the creek, and in huge ovens the wood baked to hard, black charcoal bricks that fired the iron furnace on a wooded hill in the high country.

Industry is all but gone along the East Branch. The water flows on, and the trees are still most abundant beside the creek. The woods are pretty now—the trees merely nice to look at—and that, in this world where power is borne across a terrain of technology and cement, seems quite enough.

Old mill window

Along the northern country roads, the East Brandywine is best seen from bridges. It can emerge from the forest, pass beneath the road and then flow on, determined, toward fields again where the water trickles flatly. When the current snakes again through flat woodlands, the creek sometimes retreats and deceives the roadway with an obsolete mill race in its stead. As the high ground falls away downstream, toward the Great Valley that led settlers west from the Delaware and Schuylkill, the Brandywine will chisel deep into a wooded ravine.

Maples, hemlock, mountain laurel and oak grab the soil beside the steep creek banks. Water rolls over the streambed rocks and makes them smooth, while jagged stone crops up through the surrounding earth. Rains and snow turned liquid in spring seep into the earth and slide the banks. The water turns muddy, bottomless, as it rises to bury the rocks and the tree roots.

The earth beside the creek is a sponge, damp even in midsummer, when the sky milks up a flat gray but will not nurse the fields. The valley turns the color of premature harvest, of a farmer's hay and wheat severed from the root and left purposefully to dry in the sun. Uncoiled hoses hiss and spit water across parched lawns, and all the while the creek's flowing water gently nourishes the loam, greens the jewel weed, locust tree and day lily. Haze blurs impressionistic; the goldfinch perched on a thistle is a dab of yellow oil paint, a stroke of violet.

The water first passes mills on the upper creek, built of fieldstone smoothed and mortared before the Revolution. There will be bygone mills from here to the water's confluence with larger rivers—some restored as homes or work places, others fallen to skeletal rubble, the stones returning to the earth from which they came. And the races, a host of channels that were shoveled deep long ago to deter the feisty water and control its turning of the water wheel, have dried.

Within a half mile of a dormant grist mill on the upper creek, two men earn their livings by operating neighboring sawmills—their blades powered not by the rush of water at the base of their hill, but by electricity generated miles away by huge river dams and nuclear reactors. One woodcutter saws planks and nails together industrial skids; the other, further down Lewis Mill Road, mills logs to order.

Clarence Reinhart

Wood is still abundant here, as it was for the first sawyers two hundred years ago. This land never was much good for planting, and the forests have earned their right to the northern hills. There are plenty of local trees hauled to the blade today. They are felled to clear lots to plant the houses that the remaining local farmers call "the new cash crop."

A small forest of logs is stacked beside Clarence Reinhart's mill shed, where the smell of fresh-sawn wood lingers long after the cutting is done. Since the day he built the mill, he has risen at 4:30 every morning save Sundays. He'll clamp a twenty-foot length of rock oak, cut down in its eightieth year, heave it onto the platform as though he's nudging a fence post, and then slice cleanly through the tree. Many logs ago, the machine functioned as a portable mill. Clarence and his father used to cart its long ramp and blade through the once-forested, now highly developed town of Broomall, just outside of Philadelphia, to mill wood for heavy construction.

"I was born and raised on the back door of a saw mill. I thought that was it when I was growing up. But my sons aren't in the business. They're electronic engineers," he says with a smile, "making good money." He isn't sure what he'll do with the business when he retires, because he hasn't given retirement a lot of thought. Even when the blade runs full tilt and chips fly across the noisy mill, sawing is a peaceful profession.

Clarence lives in a quiet land above the Brandywine, a land of weekend tinkerers. A neighbor down the road works his oriental garden across the rocky soil, another around the bend tools with his truck that sat out the past twenty-three years in his stone barn. And on Saturdays Clarence himself putters inside a stone house across the road from his mill—a nineteenth-century handyman's special with 16-inch stone walls. The place needed shoring up and new floorboards, but the tree-lined property provided the materials to make it sound again.

He looks toward the house. "It's kind of nice to think about, using the tree that was growing there, in the house—so it can stay on the property."

Unlike the rich, flat soil that surrounds it, the rock-scarred valley of the upper East Branch was ignored by the English settlers. It was considered the dregs of the land, unsuitable for farming, yet the Welsh and Scots, who came later to America, saw in it a comforting resemblance to their native soil.

The Welsh Quakers had first settled in the eastern part of Chester County, and laid out a 40,000-acre rectangle called The Welsh Tract. They named their towns St. Davids, Tredyffrin, and Bryn Mawr after their homeland villages, and hoped to form an autonomous barony, a government of their own. But William Penn thought otherwise and drew the Welsh under his authority. Disgruntled, they packed their trunks and moved north and west toward the edge of the Great Valley, carved from a soft limestone vein between sandstone and granite, around the year 1710. They put down new foundations north along the Brandywine, in a place they named Nantmeal—which means "sweet stream" in Welsh—and when they settled into the sandstone hills, the craggy rocks and rises became their own.

These twice-transplanted Welshmen grazed sheep on this land. They built tiny houses, maybe twenty by thirty feet, of rough-hewn logs packed with wood chips or a mortar of clay and straw, and they dug races beside the Brandywine to tame the water for mills. Through perseverance, some prospered. The local farmers, who at first shunned them, soon depended on the turning of the Welsh millers' stones to grind wheat, corn and barley to flour dust.

Mr. Greist

Abandoned sawmill

Debbie, spinning wool

Beside an obsolete dam in the village of Cupola, an old grist mill is now a house. It was built thick like a fort, and the interior, where the gears and cogs once turned the heavy millstone, is like a great hall. There was a large pond behind the dam once, where skaters could have a good run in winter before the blocks of ice were cut thick from the surface and carted off to line refrigeration houses. The pond has dried, except for a squiggle of creek, and the terrain has filled in with silt and grown over with trees and grasses.

This is East Nantmeal, where the Brandywine gently darts beneath roads, twists through forests and beside dairy farms. As it descends, controversy grows over whether the Brandywine is, in fact, a river—whether the narrow, shallow flow merits such a name. But here, miles before the feeding tributaries and the eastern run's merge with the West Branch, there is no question; it is a docile creek.

Across the road from the Cupola mill, a school teacher named Debbie Mikulak raises sheep for wool. She and her husband live in a former inn, once a stopping place for drovers *en route* to Philadelphia.

Isabella Furnace

Each spring, lambs white with youth bounce across their pen beside the creek, and a shearer comes to the farm to clip the yellowed wool from the older sheep for spinning.

Sheep are an avocation for the spinner, but their keep was a necessity for the settlers. Before shearing, the shepherds used to dip them into Brandywine pools to release the dirt and parasites from the oily wool. And when the shearing was finished, the wool washed, carded, and spun to fine yarn, they would weave tight cloth and sew breeches or heavy skirts to ward off winter chill.

The passing droves of sheep waned along these northern roads at the turn of the nineteenth century. As iron forged the expanding nation, new industry pervaded the upper East Branch. A small village emerged from the forest atop the Brandywine's gully, really a serfdom before the iron master's mansion where wives and children tended the gardens and livestock and served in the big house while the men worked in the mills and the furnace. Isabella, a furnace named like nearby Rebecca and Johanna for an iron master's wife, was an empire grown of the water's power, native ore, and the surrounding dense hardwood forests. Forests felled in this case for charcoal.

Charcoal was the means to processing iron ore, a more practical take than the precious metals that had evaded prospectors in these hills through the years. There was a legend born of Welsh Mountain of a lost silver mine, tales of the Conestoga Indians who were said to have come down from the hills with large chunks of silver to barter for goods in the general store in nearby Morgantown. For years, the white man ventured up the mountain, but there was no mine. And long after the Conestogas ventured west, hopefuls were picking at the rocky soil in search of any glitter.

The iron furnace, which rose in 1835 alongside Perkins Run as it flowed toward the larger creek, supplied the North with cannon balls during the Civil War. Isabella forged security and prosperity for the iron master, Henry Potts, and his managers, and from the workers it demanded long hours in the putrid and dangerous furnace.

When Colonel Joseph D. Potts bought the furnace in 1880, he made an effort to improve working conditions at Isabella. The prosperous civil engineer made a fortune in oil in western Pennsylvania and cleared a reported $4 million in Northern Pacific Railroad stock. He was by far the wealthiest man within miles of the upper Brandywine, and by surrounding his property with a stone wall that took two decades to build, he created more jobs. To build the miles of stone wall, workers hitched skids to a six-mule team and brought the stones down from Potts' Mine on Welsh Mountain.

When Colonel Potts died at the close of the nineteenth century, his son William completed work on the serfdom within those stone walls. The giant stone mansion he built on his two-thousand-acre estate is among the most imposing residences in Chester County. The manor "Langoma" still stands, its turrets higher than the trees atop the hill, and habit-clad women now walk across the lawn. It is a residence for older members of the Daughters of St. Mary of Providence, and it remains well hidden and alone.

The stone walls emboss the wooded hills near the former site of Isabella, where at night the orange glow of the furnace once lighted a village and charcoal dust lingered constantly in the air. The ore-crusher building atop the hill was restored in 1972 as a residence. Below it is a pile of rubble that once housed fire and billowed smoke.

Downstream, where the eastern Brandywine crosses beneath Route 82, a family bought and resurrected a general store that had long been closed. The Barneston General is a three-level wooden building with a hill of steps to the front porch. A convenience store without the plate glass and franchise license, where children sit and lick ice cream in a race against the summertime heat.

The village of Barneston, a small cluster of houses, was named for the engineer who laid out the railroad that tied the settlement to the larger market towns in the middle nineteenth century. In the center was one of the six wooden bridges that once crossed the upper creek. The bridges were erected by the county; a hundred years ago, local township budgets were too tight to afford the expensive construction costs. But the county, too, had to guard its purse strings, and before the money was allotted, local citizens had to sign a petition stating their need for a bridge—like the one signed in 1859 for Bartram's crossing along Crum Creek to the south, in which residents petitioned "a bridge here is indispensably essential."

If the bridge was, in fact, deemed indispensable by the six or so prominent residents appointed by the County Court of Quarter Sessions to review the plea, an ad in the local newspaper called for construction bids. Soon stonemasons would begin building the base of

Barneston Dry Dam

mortar and field stone and a carpenter would piece together with whittled trunnel the boards that would span the creeks for decades.

The covered wooden bridge that crossed the Brandywine at Barneston in 1855 was demolished a century later, said to be inhabited in those final years by "bats and bums." Of the ninety-eight covered bridges that once spanned the creeks of Chester County, thirteen remain. Dorlans, Lyndell, Cornog, Glenmoore, and Forrest laid their covered bridges across this creek to the south, and like the one at Barneston, they too, are gone. They too, were thought unsafe, and were burned and replaced by steel girder or concrete in the thirties and forties. Modernized.

Two decades later, in the early seventies, the covered bridge was revived as a quaint and vital relic. A local society formed in Chester County, dedicated solely to retaining the history and maintaining the covered bridges that remain.

Down the creek a quarter mile from Barneston's concrete bridge, imposing gray walls of poured concrete rise 75 feet from a virtually waterless basin. Barneston Dry Dam looks from the roadside as though it serves no useful purpose. It was designed to work silently, to reduce flood damage downstream when the thaw brings heavy runoff from the hills or a summer thunderstorm drenches the ground. The Brandywine no longer charges southward with each heavy rainfall; it is controlled neatly by a four-foot opening on the northern face of the dry dam, taken through a T of concrete that looks like nothing so much as a bridge abutment, and directed beneath the big gray wall. Twenty yards below, like an animal that has been for a brief moment penned and then set free, the Brandywine plays across the rocks and then flows on toward the woods below.

The creek hides behind the brick and wooden houses along the highway that parallels the Brandywine at Glenmoore—steep, peaked Victorians that stand stiff and high-collared against the road. People don't call this thoroughfare Creek Road these days—it is Route 282—and the staunch facades of the houses seem to stiffen in disdain at rush hour traffic.

In a brickface house along 282 lives John Shrader, who, like Calvin Smoker up in Honey Brook, collects the arrowheads the Indians discarded a few hundred years ago. Unlike Smoker, Shrader's interest goes beyond finding the bits to clean and display. Oh, of course there's that fascination with the locally abundant milky quartz, the shades of jasper, and the beauty of the tiny chisel marks worked skillfully toward a clean, sharp point, but Shrader thrills most upon envisioning the past. The artifacts are clues to that former life, as are the shelves of books that line his living room wall. To know a good piece when he sees one—like the Paleo point that poked up from plowed earth in Honey Brook some 12,000 years after the hunter carved and smoothed the stone—he studies and reads. His collection is small and selective, his display boxes labeled with brass plates that read: "Aboriginal Antiquities of Wallace Township."

Shrader once held a platform pipe carved of deep green serpentine stone from the Middle Woodland Epoch, discovered a couple of thousand years later by a boy he brought to scout the hilltop cornfield of the Devereux School just south of town. The pipe was dated 500 B.C. to 1,000 A.D., to a late Woodland culture of the Middle Atlantic region. Shrader held the smooth cold stone in his hand, and then sadly let it remain the possession of the boy who found it. He keeps a rough drawing as a reminder of his favorite relic.

The Scots who had trudged from the southern Chester County town of Nottingham along the Nanticoke Indian Path (now Route 10) in search of land, stopped in these parts. They named their village Indiantown, for the Brandywine Band of Lenape Indians who lived there. By the time of the Revolution, Glenmoore, as it would later be called, was a small hamlet with a grist mill, a blacksmith's shop and store. A century later, it was the only town to flourish along the route of the Pennsylvania Railroad that in 1854 connected Honey Brook to Downingtown with seventeen stops.

Whether directly, because of mills and commerce, or indirectly, because the railroad was graded along the creek, Glenmoore grew up from the Brandywine. The trains would bring mail, they would pick up milk, leave bread, or carry passengers beside the scenic water. By the 1890s, the town had grown to support a general store—a cobbler and miller, butchers, a Justice of the Peace, a painter, two ministers and a school teacher—and the citizens did something rather extraordinary for such a small village. They installed street lights, and each night at dusk, Levi Rice carried a small ladder to the lamp posts and lit the coal oil lamps.

The lamps have long since vanished from Glenmoore's streets, and the train's former presence is marked only by a few rotting railroad ties and decaying trestles that cross tributaries in obsolete persistence to maintain their course along the creek. A white stucco schoolhouse where a teacher drilled her students on arithmetic over a century ago is the Wallace Township Building, Glenmoore's seat of government. A quilt hangs on the eastern wall inside, framed and behind glass, because the townspeople are proud of it. Without words, its squares say nearly everything there is to know about the old town's past.

Twenty-five women each sewed a 10-by-12-inch scene from the quiet village and pieced their squares together with edgings of blue. The Glenmoore Quilt Committee presented the Community Quilt to the town at a special ceremony in 1982, when Chester County towns were celebrating the county's tricentennial. An embroidered map is sewn across one square, with street names stitched in red and blue embroidery floss. There is the old blacksmith shop, a Holstein cow, a Brandywine fisherman, and a steam train beside a house. Sandra Printer cross-stitched a poem about the Lenni-Lenape burial site. The tiny Xs spell:

> Under Grass sod by the woodland.
> Neath the spreading Chestnut Tree.
> Buried all their fallen tribesmen
> And their trinkets pipes and fee.
> by Ada Flemington
> 1915-1978

Beneath the poem are cross-stitch renderings of the relics found by archaeologists as they excavated the grave—a brass button, clay pipes, gun flints, silver heart pin, and glass beads. When the Indians buried the prized relics with their dead, they were burying their heritage on the land. Even gold could not have paid for the forests they lost to farmers, and for the damming of the creek where they had once dragged grapevine nets to capture fish.

The quilt also includes a square of the 1849 Cornog covered bridge. It was fitted together with board and tree nail before the carpenter moved on to build his next five miles upstream in Barneston. The bridge, with its rickety 82-foot span and a 14-foot roadway too narrow for passing cars, was taken down in 1925 and replaced with the $7,000

Glenmoore Quilt

steel girder County Bridge No. 137.

The most distinctive of the Brandywine's overhanging trees, the sycamore, is depicted on the quilt as well. It is bright with green and yellow calico leaves that shade the Fairview Presbyterian Church, which is of white cloth, with a blue sky and terry cloth clouds. Twenty members left the crowded Forks of the Brandywine Presbyterian along the West Branch to form this church half a mile east of Glenmoore proper. The white stucco church stands imposing as it did 150 years ago, cutting a stark silhouette against the sky.

The brown wooden gates of Springton Manor, a farm granted to William Penn, fill another square on Glenmoore's quilt. England was still largely under feudalism when King George II settled his debt to Penn by granting him 10,000 out of every 100,000 acres of land in these hills. Springton Manor, one of eight manors set aside in Chester County by his family for proprietary use, encompassed nearly all of Wallace Township and parts of West Brandywine, Honey Brook and West Nantmeal. Penn requested a survey of the sprawling land in 1700, and nearly thirty years later, after his death, the tract was charted at more than eight thousand acres.

The colony's Secretary of Propriety tried to force a band of early settlers, with supposed squatters' rights, off the land reserved by the Penn family. But the Scotch-Irish who ventured to America from Ulster, who were by temperament the antithesis of Quaker calm and German thrift, took the land available and dared anyone to try to move them. The Scotch-Irish settlers descended from English-speaking lowland Scots—Presbyterians who had settled in northern Ireland, County Ulster, after the English conquest. Many pushed up to the northern Brandywine after settling in New Castle, Delaware. Like the Welsh, they found the land was right to raise sheep, and sheered the wool to spin and weave. They were fiercely independent. It is said that there was not one Tory amidst their numbers. As they arrived in the valley last, they took the dregs of the farmland, but the Scotch-Irish stature rose when they put their all into the Revolution. Quakers and even the German sects were neutral if not pacifists.

Some of the Scots gave up the fight to hold the Manor land, though, and headed south again, toward the Susquehanna, Maryland's Cumberland Valley, and Virginia. Belligerence paid off for others, as Springton Manor was divided into 200-acre parcels, as recorded on a

Fairview Presbyterian

map dated 1788, and shares meted out to those who had cleared the fields.

The Scotch-Irish found the German settlers in the valley miserly and unfriendly. The Germans thought the English lazy farmers, and far too worldly. For their part, the English snubbed the Scotch-Irish, whom they considered ignorant peasants. Yet, despite such religious and cultural cleavage, Quakers joined Presbyterians to build schools, Germans helped Scotch-Irish to raise barns, and all worked to smooth the edges of a rough wilderness in a new nation.

Following the division of land at Springton, the manor itself was passed on within families, in more recent years to a number of gentleman farmers, and then to its last private owner, Eleanor Bartol. Ultimately she preserved the farm by endowing Springton Manor as a public land trust. The elegant white house was vacant and had fallen from grace, the huge barn with its wood-shingled roof drooping down toward the ground was in need of repair, and the surrounding buildings seemed destined for ruin when Forward Lands, the securing trust, sold the property to Chester County. A new gate now opens wide before the aged fields and buildings and Springton Manor Farm is a public park now, owned by the Chester County Parks and Recreation Commission.

To return the farm to its original state, the Parks Commission compiled a list of Things to Do that was pages long and required a budget of nearly $3 million. Acre by acre, piece by piece, they have begun to replenish the soil, and repair the shingles. It is a working farm now with pigs and goats to pet, chickens to feed, rows of vegetables, and the traditional makings of a nineteenth-century rural manor. Two giant oaks spread their branches toward the clouds and out across the ground. They are living, growing antiques that have survived the settling of this land, and the clearing of the fields. They have watched the farm prosper and fall, and now they share in its rejuvenation.

On Opening Day at Springton Manor, the day the public was invited to see the new park and its old-time ways. Roland Woodward, Sr., a farmer from Pocopson, stood atop a horse-powered wheat thresher to demonstrate the county historical society's exhibit of antique farm equipment. He spoke through a megaphone, directing his crew through their first demonstration, the earliest method of flailing the chaff by hand. Phil St. John, Bill Evans, Ira Hicks, and the other members of the Chester County Farm and Home Antiques Association still remember working rows of corn and wheat before the combine changed things. That was why they were using the fragile antiques that day, showing bygone methods to the group that gathered around the noisy machines.

The machines grew louder chronologically—from the thump, thump of Lawrence Waltman's scythe-like hand thresher to the burp and putt of the Champion thresher, to the roaring combine. Nine out of ten people in America earned a living from the soil when Penn first opened these fields—farmers worked quietly then down the rows, threshing the wheat by hand. Marshall Jones fed a fistful of wheat through his sweep power thresher, a machine used by farmers at the turn of the century. At that time, only sixty out of one hundred Americans were farming. In 1937, the year combines came to Chester County and revolutionized the farming process, just fifteen people per hundred were earning a living off the land. Today there are only two farmers for every one hundred Americans.

As the work goes on at Springton Manor, it is certain that the most beautiful part of the farm cannot be improved upon. The manor is edged all about with a dark and leafy forest. Queen Anne's lace crystalizes across the wispy meadows, along with the delicate violet of rough-leaved asters and the faded blue chickory. In high branches beside a tiny spring-fed pond on the eastern edge of the Manor, cicadas, locusts and jays intensify the heat with their summertime drones. Young frogs scoot into the small pond, disturb the minnows and send shiny blue dragonflies from between the cattails. Swallows glide speedily above the water's flat surface, scoop a second's worth of water into their beaks and dart up toward the sky. The pond is jarred, and the reflection of trees fractures and forms moving lines across the flatness like venetian blinds tapping in the breeze.

The water frosts over in winter, the cattails become brittle and break on the stalk, and frogs burrow into the mud and shut down with the coldness. Then, just before the spring thaw, before the ground becomes soft again, or the trees push open their buds through stiffened branches, is the sugaring.

The maple trees were planted 175 years ago to form the scenic drive to the mansion at Springton Manor. Norman Simmons, a park employee who helped to rebuild the farm, works through the late winter tapping the wrinkled trees to make syrup. In early March his sap

Farm Demonstration, Springton Manor

joins a yearly sugar maple festival that draws hundreds in for a breakfast of pancakes, sausages and fresh syrup.

Simmons hooked a pail made from coffee can and wire over the metal spike he had tapped through the rough bark of a sugar maple. "The spike has to go in two-and-a-half to three inches. No more," he said. "If you go into the heartwood, you kill the tree." The transplanted New Englander—a Hartford native who ventured to Pennsylvania forty years ago to break horses after a murmuring heart kept him from enlisting in the army—knows his syrup.

"When I came, they had gotten a bunch of literature and all the new fangdangled ways that they have," he said, his breath fogging the bitter March air as he unhooked a full can from the tree, "and I had the old way." And like most Connecticut Yankees, when Simmons finds a method that works well, he's not about to look for anything different. Take the new sap spouts. "You might say they're a little simpler," said Simmons, "possibly a little cheaper. I would say the only advantage is they have the hooks." But endurance? "You hit 'em with a mallet and they crinkle. The old ones would last you near about a hundred years."

At the start of the season, the second week of February, the sap is strong—thirty-three gallons will yield a gallon of syrup. Soon the run is slower, the sap weaker, and he finds he must boil down forty buckets for a gallon of syrup, and finally the water turns a milky white and he knows to pull the spikes from the bark. "When that sap is ready to go up and supply the branches," Norman said, "that sap turns to milk. You can only take so much and the trees will shut themselves off. They won't give you any more. The good Lord knew what he was doing. He put a stopping point on everything," he said.

Norman Simmons was setting his own stopping point. He has stopped going to the crowded syrup festivals, and has adopted the role of Sap-Boiler Emeritus. "I let the younger ones go into it. They're twenty or thirty years younger than the old man here and I figure I've done my share of it," he says. "They figure the same way. I'm still teaching 'em. They made a few mistakes on it this year, but they have to learn, too."

A steady creek called Indian Run edges the Manor before joining the Brandywine a short distance downstream. Together the tributaries—Perkins Run, Culbertson Run, North Branch and Indian Run—carry water from the wooded hills and down hemlock-capped

Page 46: Springton Oak

ridges to feed the Brandywine. The streams may be overly zealous in spring, charging muddy water into the larger creek, raising the flow toward houses and up beside roads. But in summer, the rocks rise parched from the stream beds, and drought threatens the communities further down the creek.

The largest water supply project along the Brandywine is Marsh Creek, a 535-acre, man-made lake that formed in 1969 from the slow swampwater that was once called the Black Brandywine. It is a state park now, and a county drought control for the Brandywine, releasing water as it is needed to quench parched municipalities downstream during the arid days of summer. The brightly colored sails of small boats and windsurfer boards look from the hill above like petals in a basin. Fishermen cast for perch and bass above the dam in summer, and drop their jigger lines through ice cut through with auger in the off season.

New houses cluster around the water now, and below the lake, beneath its murky waters, are the foundations of old dwellings—farms, mainly, and a few stores, that formed a community called Milford Mills.

"Used to be you knew everybody within a few miles," Howard Trego says, looking toward the new neighborhood alongside his property. "Now you don't know your next door neighbor." Howard and his wife Margaret live in a mobile home behind their son's house. He is 76 years old, and with time he has lost the longing for his house and farm that once sprawled in the valley where the lake is now. He had bought the 100-acre dairy farm, just a half mile from his childhood home, in 1953. He checked his traps in the morning for skunks, possums, fox, and coon, and drained the cows' udders. Then he would pack the fresh milk onto a wagon and truck it to the next town called Lyndell, where the men at the village store helped load the canisters onto trains bound for Philadelphia. Trego would stop in and see what his friends at the paper mill were up to, and then he would pick up some bread, brought to town on the same train that carried off his milk, and return home.

Howard Trego's children were grown when he got the letter about the dam; he was going to have to move to higher ground because Milford Mills was at the base of the valley that would become Marsh Creek. "None of us wanted to sell, but they come in and said they want to take it. It's all right, there's no use condemnin' it now. We had no choice, and I'd say we got a fair price," he says. "It was bad at first, and then it wasn't, 'cause the whole country's gettin' out of farming." He and his neighbors picked up everything that wasn't fastened down and moved off the farms, and in 1969, those who stayed nearby watched the valley fill with water and become a lake.

Larkin's Bridge spanned the creek that once cut across the valley sixty feet below the lake water. Its impending demise raised quite a stir when the flooding began, and the covered bridge was transplanted, like Howard Trego, above the water line. Today it is on high ground along the lake's northern shore, well removed from any road, leading nowhere in particular, but nonetheless preserved.

Lyndell Store, marking where the road from Marsh Creek meets the Brandywine, has been around these parts longer than Mr. Trego. When the railroad was running, it purveyed general merchandise, things like brooms and mousetraps, bread, milk, hats, soaps and liniments. Now the owner stocks the shelves with "what sells." If it's not junk food or fishing supplies, he doesn't have it. The store beside the creek is a lure to hook fishermen—as enticing to a sportsman as mayfly larvae wriggling atop a trout pool. The cases are filled with cubed processed cheese, mealie worms, garden worms, large and small earthworms, and corn. On the shelves there are fluorescent rubber worms—dayglow green, orange, violet—that look nothing remotely like anything a fish has seen in a hatchery, or in the Brandywine, before Opening Day.

The anticipation begins the first week in March, when local fishermen join the fish commissioner to drive alongside the big trout truck, freshly loaded at a nursery upstate. They gently scoop nets into the frothy tank, turn the 10-inch catch into white pails, and the gray trout slosh and swim in tight circles around the slick lining. The men empty the fish one by one into the deeper cool water, where sunlight dapples the surface through naked branches and minnows twist and dart in the translucence between the rocks.

On that first day of the season, always the first Saturday after April 11, members of the Brandywine Trout Association, the West Chester Fish and Game Club, West Caln Sportsman's Club and the hundreds of other fishermen line up along the creeks and cast their lines, being careful not to tangle with their neighbors.

His badge may just say Water Conservation Officer, but the locals say that Ray Bednarchik has as much power (if not more) as a state trooper. He packs a pistol, has a fully outfitted patrol car, and is

authorized to write speeding tickets, though he says he never feels a need to. He's more interested in the water, "enforcing boat laws," he says, "working outdoors and protecting the wildlife."

Bednarchik's beat spans the Chester County watershed from Honey Brook to the Delaware border and he is an avid fisherman himself, pursuing trout and smallmouth bass not with cheese but with self-tied flies. The official season ends Labor Day, and the waterways conservation officer catches up on paperwork through the winter.

The water below Lyndell is obscured later in spring by leaves. Where it is wide, it is moving yet silent, it sings and glistens as it drops or turns over rocks, and then it is still again. Struble Trail, like the lake to the north, was named for Robert Struble, Sr., a county commissioner who supported acquisition of land for public use. In spring, it is the site of a five-mile race, and in winter, skiers take to the skimpiest of snowfalls to glide above the Brandywine's banks.

Chester County's Commissioners dedicated the trail in 1979. Built on an abandoned railroad right-of-way, it ends just before Dorlan's Mill Road. Some day, the county parks department hopes it will continue north past Lyndell, Cornog and Glenmoore, past Springton Manor and Struble Lake, for a total of sixteen miles. Today it is three miles long. It has hit a snag. The county has been unable to negotiate land use beyond the parking lot of the Shryock Brothers paper mill that borders the creek, said to be one of the oldest continually operating paper makers in America.

On the south end of the trail the creek tumbles out of the gorge toward Downingtown. An industrial town, with old paper mills in its center, and hi-tech manufacturers on its outskirts. In the second quarter of the eighteenth century, Germans moved to the valley from the middle Rhine valley and German-speaking Switzerland. They had first settled in Germantown and Montgomery County and then moved west to Chester County, drawn by word of fertile land. Like the Quakers, they had strong and independent religious views, and prospered.

After the creek tumbles out of the woods to widen across this valley that once ran emigrants toward Lancaster from Philadelphia, it changes character. It is flat, slow water from here on; it is no longer the cool, aerated trout water of the north. Further south the Brandywine will soon be somewhat navigable; deep enough to float the long, flat

Page 50: Marsh Creek

21, 1988. A log house was being moved, and it was a media event. It was unassuming once, just a little house beside the road—a shelter at one time for the Downing family for whom the borough was named. The little log cabin had gripped its foundations for more than 250 years, but it looked all wrong after progress came to town. Like it was leaping toward the busy state highway, backed up against the wall of a car dealership, threatened perhaps by the rising water of the Brandywine. For four years, the miniature house, a symbol of the settling of a nation, had been a burden. An issue of many a municipal meeting, and the centerpiece of a citizen action group.

Townspeople thought the house looked cramped, and the vibrations from trucks a few yards away made its old window panes rattle. They formed the Friends of the Log House committee. A structural engineer was brought in to measure the effects of traffic vibration and fumes, people went to Harrisburg to lobby, and a six-person restoration committee was appointed.

There were snags—had they moved the house further from the road, they would have lost a sycamore tree in addition to the pine they had to fell. More importantly, law states that a building is debarred from the National Historic Register when lifted from its foundation and moved too far from where it was first built. But a conservation architect convinced the state preservation board that its location was contributing to its deterioration, and that the cabin had to be moved.

With shovels the crew dug out the foundation that was set in place in 1720, and when they jacked up the 60-ton house not so much as a piece of plaster fell from the fireplace. While the crowd strained against the chain for a better look, the movers set the cabin down upon a sand pad to help control shock from passing traffic. The first floor settled in about a foot and a half above the 100-year flood plain.

After the cabin was moved, people began to wonder. It was moved only thirty feet or so. Why all the hubbub? The endless meetings and the fund raisers? Sure, it was a long time coming, and the people of Downingtown were glad to see the house have its day, but it seemed the move was actually toward the creek and back from the road only a few feet.

"I'm disillusioned," a man said from the crowd. "It will be out of the way of the road, but if they ever widen the Lincoln Highway like they're supposed to, it will be right back against the road." The mayor walked by with a blackened utensil, quipping something about George Washington's breakfast spoon. Yes, it was a historic day for the historic house, and once it was resituated and a team of experts replaced its rotting timbers and gave the 270-year-old house a new life, it would be a source of community pride.

Dixie Collins Shirk watched the move, recalling a hazy image from her childhood, of a woman scrubbing the floor of the cabin while her nine children ran about the yard. She doesn't remember why she was at the cabin, or how the small house accommodated the large family, but she thought of how she always took the log cabin in her home town for granted. Until today.

"It looks so proud sitting there. It looks so proud," she says, her voice straining over the growl of machinery. "I'm afraid the water still comes up here, but I'm so glad they didn't move it out of the way so that you can't see it."

Mrs. Shirk points toward the Methodist Church across the street, freshly wounded with a wrecking ball, its gaping sides revealing sanctuary and brightly painted Sunday School rooms. "I'm sorry about that. And they tore down the Lutheran Church, too. You hate to see things go," she says. "I think they're going to use it for a parking lot."

The Brandywine flows behind the place where Mrs. Shirk feared a parking lot would spread; the dirt lot was actually filled with a new office building. The creek passes behind brick duplex houses and then on toward Johnstown, the Italian neighborhood at the edge of town where, in 1934, "Cappy" DiGiovantonio and his friends first aimed their .22-caliber rifles at the bullfrogs that splashed along these banks.

As kids, Cappy and his gang would grab the frogs from the water with their hands, but after the hunting got serious, and they began taking shots at the amphibians, Arthur Petrilla, the corner grocer in town, had an idea. "Give 'em to me, guys," he said. "I'll put the legs in my freezer and we'll have a party at the end of the year." There were 15 young men at that first get-together. More parties followed each summer until some of the boys went off to fight World War II, and when they returned, the frog leg affair was formalized—guaranteed each year the first Thursday in August.

The boyhood pastime launched a legend, and a members-only club more exclusive, perhaps, than the Social Register. Seven hundred men strong, and they say you practically have to be born into it or join the

Pages 56,57: Brandywine at Downingtown

waiting list that grows more quickly than it shrinks, because a member has to die or move out of town before a new one can join. The Amphibious Order of Frogs meets once a year. Its function: Nothing more than to throw a terrific party devoted to devouring several hundred pounds of frog legs amongst friends.

Cappy DiGiovantonio was 82 years old and the guest of honor at the 54th anniversary meeting of the Amphibious Order in the summer of 1988. The frogs no longer come from the Brandywine, they come from Bangladesh, and Order members from as far as California and Florida. The Reverend George Schneider, down from Our Lady of Consolation Church in Parkesburg, delivered the invocation in the back lot at St. Anthony's Lodge, thanking God for the feast and remembering the passing of past members. There were frog legs enough that every man could have six or seven, and the feast went on long after the sun set.

Just south of town, a sewage treatment plant called the Downingtown Regional Water Pollution Control Center has grown with the rapid development in the late seventies and eighties of the once rural towns that hem in Downingtown. Its sewage capacity has been raised from four to seven to twelve million gallons a day and will be raised again as the municipalities to the north and east continue to hook new houses to the sewer lines. At times the plant's effluent constitutes half of the creek's total flow, a growing concern to water authorities and users down stream.

The Davey Paper Company has been in operation on the southern edge of town since 1840. It first set up shop on the eastern bank because of the water, but the company no longer puts anything into the creek, nor does it take water out. It recycles sixty tons of used paper a day, paper that is first ground into pulp using a huge blender that also screens out undesirable plastic and metal contaminants. The pulp is then pressed and dried, to make hard covers for books.

Below Downingtown, a rusted iron railroad trestle, erected in the early 1900s to carry the Pennsylvania Railroad's low-grade freight line high above the river-cut valley, looks as narrow and menacing as a high wire. Far below, the Brandywine twists parallel to the iron trestle, and turns south, where Gibson's Bridge—the only covered bridge that remains of the eleven along the East Branch—crosses at Harmony Hill Road. This one, made of wood and secure because of its barn-like construction, was saved in 1959. The commissioners who agreed to

Log house, Brandywine

Cows, Georgia Farm

Sycamore beside the pasture

build it in 1872 were immortalized by the marble marker set into the southeast stone wing wall.

C. MARSHALL INGRAM
NATHAN GRIM
ALFRED WOOD
County Commissioners

Bridges, both old and new, have traditionally been inscribed with the names of the commissioners who approved them. A practice thought odd by West Chester lawyer Wilmer W. MacElree, who walked these banks at the turn of the century to write two books about the Brandywine. Upon stopping for a moment to read the names inscribed on a bridge, he wrote in *Down the Eastern and Up the Black Brandywine* (published in 1906), "You ask yourself the question, 'Is it a love of glory or a desire to furnish needful information to posterity, that induces Commissioners to carve their names upon the date-stone of bridges?'"

Heraclitus, a ponderer of ancient days, once said you can't step into the same river twice. As the Brandywine flows south, elements are put into the water, and elements are removed. The fishermen who put trout into the creek upstream and in nearby Valley Creek will fish them out again. Some of the wastewater and sewage that was treated and put into the Brandywine at Downingtown will be removed again a few miles downstream.

When it first reaches the treatment plant at Ingram's Mill, the Brandywine is not nearly the same creek that we saw emerge as a spring from rocks on Welsh Mountain. The seven million gallons of water that flow east through a fibrous system of pipes and spray from faucets in West Chester are not at all like the sweet, cool liquid that Al Given drinks from the cup he keeps in a tree. West Chester's water, which has passed through pastures and the back lots of industry, is taken in just a mile down from the Downingtown sewage treatment plant and requires another powerful treatment here. The process begins with a method efficient and long proven. Water is raised to the pump station much as the water in Rome was raised 2,300 years ago, by the turning of huge Archimedes' screws. The long, threaded cylinders, named for the Greek mathematician who invented the process, draw water from the creek below to the plant's holding ponds.

From there, the water is directed to flocculation and sedimentation basins, then it is treated with chlorine, and finally directed to the clear well. Purified, colorless as it was at its birth from the rock, but now smelling of chlorine, the water travels through 120 miles of pipeline beneath surrounding towns. Then it's down the drains and through sewer lines once more to another sewage treatment plant before it's returned to the Brandywine downstream at Taylor Run.

The East Branch passes beneath the arches of Copes Bridge from the woodland, beneath the Strasburg Road that will soon cross the other Brandywine along its western course. A whitened stand of sycamores welcomes the water to pasture land, and then the current curves abruptly east. It must veer off, because the southwest bank pushes up beneath a granite sheer, a cliff several yards above the water that was named, so some say, for a legendary Indian girl.

Deborah's Rock is the tangible evidence of a legend that has been retold, and discounted by historians, for more than a hundred years. When the Lenape Indians left Chester County for lands west, Deborah, along with a few others of her tribe, remained. According to one legend, a settler's son, smitten with her beauty, seized her one moonlit night and she broke away and fled down a wooded path. She followed the dim trail until it ended high above the rushing water of the creek. There she looked down, her choice was death or dishonor, and she plunged into the stream.

According to another legend, the young princess Deborah, in this case the daughter of a Nanticoke chief, was courted by two braves named Wawaset and Kaucke. Deborah's father and her people would not accept her true love, Wawaset, as he was the son of the chief of a hostile tribe. Nonetheless, the lovers eloped and en route to Wawaset's people they were intercepted and Kaucke killed Wawaset. A very distraught Deborah was carried back to her tribe where a marriage to Kaucke was arranged that night. She stole away, climbed high atop this rocky cliff over the Brandywine, and threw herself down into the waters below and was drowned.

As with so many of the romantic legends that have arisen from the Brandywine Valley, Deborah's sad tale is highly debatable. One historian will put money, instead, on the less sensational theory that the rock was named not for an Indian maiden, but for Deborah Taylor, daughter of the Quaker settler who built the house that stands a short

Pages 64,65: Bluebells

branch to the west, a creek that has meanwhile led an active life of its own, that brings experience and strength to the remainder of the Brandywine River.

But here, the single East Branch winds lightly through fields of grazing horses. "There he is. See? He's running toward the Brandy-wine." The hounds have stirred a fox from cover in the fields below Allerton Farm. Each Christmas morning a group of bundled, hatted, booted people gather here to watch the Brandywine Hunt assemble for the chase. Some of the riders today are grandchildren of those who rode the first hunt, established in 1901 when Charles E. Mather, a Philadelphia insurance broker, moved his pack to a farm downriver near Lenape. On this cold Christmas morning, some members forgo formal attire in the name of practicality. While on-lookers raise cups of eggnog, the horses set off across whitened fields.

Just before the branches meet, above a crossing once known as Buffington's Ford, a giant oak inhabits an island below Shaws' Bridge. Gnarled with the passing of two hundred winters, its roots tug the eastern creek's final island from the water. It is the tree's way of bidding the East Branch farewell.

Cupola, Blue Rock Farm

Brandywine Hounds at Allerton Farm

Allerton Farm

WEST BRANCH

Twin tributaries nursed by thread-like feeder brooks join currents to form the West Brandywine. The creek is born a mile or so from the East. It runs briefly parallel to the East Branch, then breaks away and distances itself by miles. The West Branch assumes its own identity, and life along these banks is notably different.

The creek begins its journey through hardwood forest, passes alongside farms, and mills, some gone and some remaining. Its power has pushed through the twentieth century; the water passes through a race beside a black mammoth steel factory, then winds slowly down again through peaceful culverts, preparing to merge with the eastern creek and form a single river.

On the Brandywine's southernmost Amish farm, a moving barricade of cows brings drivers to a halt along the road that separates their stone-pillared barn from green pastureland. The mercury has climbed above 90 again, and the cows' patchy, black-and-white bodies pass slowly across the pavement like a braking cargo train. Beyond the crossing, where a farmer peers from beneath his straw brim patiently awaiting the last Holstein through the pasture gate, the western creek has entered the woods.

To meet Icedale and South Birdell, Beaver Dam Road climbs the first stone bridge that arcs up and over the creek. The water edges back a brief distance from the roadway, where it takes cover behind the leaves and brush until it spreads out toward the valley just above Coatesville. Two Log Run, the tiny brook that spills into the creek above the cow pasture, seems to nourish this rich, dense, more forested West Branch Brandywine. Like the East Branch, the West outgrows its subtler earthen run and widens over rough stone.

It passes a rugged rise known as the Baron Hills. Some spell it Barren, which may be as fitting a name, for not a lot has changed here since the late-eighteenth century. The higher slopes are capped only with a dense covering of trees and shrubs. To the country farmers and the people in town, the land on the ridge and to the north on Welsh Mountain was a wilderness as wild and wooly as any. In the 1880s, the infamous Abe Buzzard and his gang of rustlers hid out in these hills between cattle raids on area farms and trips to Wilmington and Philadelphia to sell their take. Long after he was behind bars in the Lancaster jail, travelers on the wooded roads would shudder at a breaking stick. And they said the upper Brandywine headwaters grew snakes "as big as stovepipes."

An immigrant settled at the edge of these hills below Welsh Mountain in the 1780s. While on a mission, some say, from the Hapsburg Emperor Joseph II to found a market for Belgian goods in Philadelphia. His name alone must have aroused the curiosity of his neighbors—Jacob Francis Frederick Engenue Nugent, Baron deBellen Bertholf. But he simply penned his signature Baron deBellen Bertholf and the local tax collector had him down as "Baron De Billion." Together with his wife, a woman with an equally impressive name—Jeanne-Marie-Teresa de Cartro Toldeo—the baron had lived in Philadelphia, laying the groundwork for a trade treaty and reporting back to the Empire on the financial, social, and commercial structure of this fledgling country as they saw it from the busy port.

The couple soon grew tired of the crowded streets, and trekked as far west of the city as possible without venturing too far into the wilderness. These hills just north of the Great Valley are where they chose to stop. They carved out an estate called "Head of Little Brandywine" beside the West Branch in Cambridge. They hired several servants, built their own blacksmith shop and brick kiln, and cultivated a botanical garden where the baron experimented with European plants.

Baron de Billion had few neighbors, and he liked it that way. Today people have the same idea—to find a plot away from the fast pace of city and suburb and build a dream home. Things have grown more complicated since the baron's day; unexplored territory doesn't exist and development, anywhere in this watershed, will somehow impact another property—a farm pond or a spring that nourishes the larger waterways.

Inside the municipal buildings of these rural townships, planning commissioners line front tables to oversee the inevitable building across farmland. And with the advent of each proposed subdivision, townspeople concerned for their properties fill metal folding chairs and wait their turns to speak at public hearings. At times the disputes between developers and township officials, residents and state or federal agencies, grow heated. The conflict is generally over preservation—preserving a field, a rural buffer around one's home, a forest, or even a lake.

After Struble and Marsh Lake were created by man, given to the landscape by the rerouting of the Brandywine and its feeders, the water of Icedale Lake, here on the West Branch, was drained away. The basin was first dammed so that its waters would freeze, and its upper crust could be cut into blocks by a Wilmington ice company, mortared with sawdust, and carted to the city by the passing trains. Long after refrigeration froze out the Consumer's Ice Company and made Icedale's initial purpose obsolete, the lake lingered. It remained a shimmering waterhole where young boys fished in late afternoon, and couples spread picnics on summer weekends.

Through the years, the lake grew old gracefully with the passing of summers, except for the spillway at its southern end, where the stones and earth began to crumble under the water's weight. It was as if the water shunned retention in its southward race. Eventually, the Pennsylvania Fish Commission demolished the West Branch spillway. In 1984, it let loose the water that had filled the basin since it was

Ice

dammed seventy-one years before.

The draining was necessary, like putting an injured animal out of its misery; but to the owners of the houses that overlooked Icedale's glassy reflection, the coup de grace was cruel and insensitive. At first word of the drainage plan they had gathered at the Brandywine Woods Campground, named their action group SILT (Save Icedale Lake Today), and collected hundreds of signatures to petition the state to repair the injured spillway. Nonetheless, in less than a month, the yellow bulldozers were parked beside the bridge and a Fish Commission spokesman told the people his agency had no choice; the bridge would wash out atop the straining banks if the lake was not drained. And so the earth movers brought the spillways down and loosed the water, and that July the mud baked and cracked where the trees had once gazed down at their reflected images.

Now the basin is a grassy marsh, its forty acres spongy and green with spiky wetland plants. The Brandywine found its own narrow banks again after Icedale's final pools soaked into the earth. The water darts through the weeds, beneath the road, to forest again. There it can be seen only from the jeep trail remnants of an extinct railroad track.

In 1988, the County Parks and Recreation administrators worked to persuade the County Commissioners to approve purchase of the abandoned Conrail line that parallels the West Branch from Coatesville to Honey Brook. The hidden trails will be smoothed and paved with fine-ground stone. A trail like Struble on the East Branch, where people can hike through the fields of the linear park, ride bicycles along its smooth path, and, come winter, ski beside the icy water.

The county politicians were lobbied by those who wanted the park, and those who feared the public access would invade their own country solitude and bisect their farms. The Commissioners knew that either decision would stir anger in the peaceful valley, but went ahead in hopes that a trail built on the $1 right-of-way would preserve another open space amidst a shrinking countryside.

A mile south of Icedale, the West Branch Brandywine resurfaces from the northern woods to feed a small pond. A stone mill and a colony of peeling white clapboard and cinder block buildings sprout from the green, moist plain like mushrooms. The creek is channeled through a mill race—a dormant run that John Hatfield carved in order to grind grain in his sturdy stone mill. The race was maintained by his sons until they shut the mill down at the close of World War I. A

Presbyterian church in Philadelphia bought Brandamore mill in 1933 and built dormitories and outbuildings across the fields. The congregation positioned a few white wooden chairs beside the lazy pond, strung a basketball net on a central pole, and named their summertime retreat the Old Mill Bible Conference.

In time the Bible Conference closed, the buildings were sold, and the sanctuary stood empty until an itinerant pastor brought his fledgling congregation to Old Mill for a summer not long ago. "I get churches going, and then I move on. But I broke down and cried when I first walked into that sanctuary," the Reverend Marty Lewis says one late summer day. "I looked at this and I thought about the thousands of people who were saved out here, and the thousands who were called to preach." People from around the country would call or stop by, just wondering what had come of the place. They'd return to find the utopia had slowly decayed to this state where even the dreamer would waver between thoughts of renovation and wrecking ball.

Reverend Lewis left the mill near the end of summer, packed up the Living Word Baptist Church and moved to a Downingtown hotel conference room. He left behind little more than the church's newly painted sign alongside the creek's scuttle below Baron's Hill Road. Along the bottom of the sign, the reverend's words proclaim: "A Going Church for a Coming LORD."

On an eastern hill above golden barley fields, the Forks of the Brandywine Presbyterian Church (the mother church of Fairview on the East Branch) pushes its spire up toward the sky. East Branch actually meets West some twelve miles south of here, but the church was named in a day when a typical member would never see the merge. During the eighteenth century, "The Forks" denoted the entire terrain between the headwaters and the merge of East Branch with West between Wawaset and Lenape.

In wintertime, the air is crisp and black when Joan Rigg turns off Hibernia Road, just south of the church, and pulls up beside a farmhouse-turned-post-office where she is the postmistress. In this diffused village called Brandamore, named a hundred years ago for an early postmaster's wife, there is no rural delivery. The trains stopped running the mail in 1949, and it wasn't long ago that the village post office comprised fifty boxes on Mrs. Rigg's mother-in-law's front porch. Still, the post office is the only enterprise in town, and Joan is probably the best-known Brandamore resident for her daily contact with the 220 boxholders here.

She comes out of the house every morning to hoist the flag up a pole and into the chill air, ties down the line, and returns to the back room to begin sorting the day's mail into slots. She took on a slew of new customers when the Brandamore Woods subdivision went up where a cornfield used to be across the grove. Brandamore is on the southern edge of one of Chester County's major concentrations of actively farmed land. In 1950 there were 358,000 farmed acres in the county. By 1980, that number had dropped to 220,000 acres. For the first time, there was more land that could be called "urban or suburban" than "agricultural or rural."

Then, the real depletion of open land began with a rush of development throughout the county. By 1988, Chester County was losing open space to development at a rate of nearly a hundred acres a day. The raw soil that provides a means of groundwater recharge, the crops that produce oxygen and help to purify the air, have been depleted with each new subdivision. The County Commissioners created the Chester County Agricultural Development Council in 1980 to try to retain farmland. They have encouraged Agricultural Districts, with deed restrictions through purchase of land development rights. Along with land preservation groups, sportsmen, and determined farmers, they have fought to preserve the many Brandamores across the valley.

Just under 140 empty boxes remain at Joan Rigg's post office, room for a little growth along Brandamore Road. The boxholders who stop in to chat have come to expect the growth. They've watched the fields fill in around Brandamore and the grove sprout lumber frames. But for now, there are plows furrowing the soil across hills to the south and not bulldozers. For now barley, wheat, hay and soybeans cover the land, and as the fields lay flat and open to the sun, the creek holds its cover beneath the trees.

In a shaded twist of woods an old sycamore tree grips the stream bed, its knobby roots exposed and swirling like a snaking current. The roots above the creek look dry and dead, but beneath the rocks they are well-quenched. The old timer's leaves are green with health, smaller than those on meadow sycamores for these roots are sufficiently nourished. One has to wonder how the tender seedling survived the current and the drenching water. How it thrived and grew

to join the raw, wizened senior citizens of the forest.

Some of the trees in this county park called Hibernia were saplings in the late eighteenth century, when Samuel Downing was converting pig iron to bar iron in his forge. Their stout trunks have fared better for the years than the iron master's stone and mortar buildings. Downing's forge hides beside the creek, three of its stone walls crouching loosely in a dense cover of vine and brush where they were once warmed by the glowing furnace.

This land was for more than a century an active forge. Its most prosperous iron master, a man named Charles Brooke, bought the property in 1821 and supervised two forges and heating furnaces, a rolling mill, grist mill, and several houses amid the forest. Although Brooke's elaborate gardens and orchards have long grown over, several of the millworkers' houses of the Hibernia Iron Works have been restored. Collectively they are documented as the Hatfield-Hibernia Historic District on the National Register of Historic Places.

At the turn of the century, a pair of cast-iron lion heads arrived to guard the entrance to the 800-acre manor here. They were the motif of a Philadelphia real estate lawyer, a Colonel Franklin Swayne, who converted Hibernia to a gentleman's estate—a place to raise sheep, harvest ice, farm, and build stables and kennels for fox hunting. After

Stream sycamore

Winter, Hibernia

his marriage to an English actress (undoubtedly a woman he met on one of his twenty-nine trips to England), Swayne added a wing to the Hibernia mansion so that the two could host a Christmas party. That would be the first and last gala thrown in the extravagant ballroom. The couple divorced shortly afterwards, and Swayne in his older years willed the property not to a wife but to his cousin, Mary Skerritt Matteson.

Meanwhile, the rolling mills had fallen to rock and mortar dust, and the buildings that remained upright invited tramps and welcomed bats through open windows to the rotting eaves. Mary Matteson may never have seen the ice clump in globules along the Brandywine, or the way the snow frosted the forge and clung to the trees like white foliage after a storm. This was for her a summer home. But her legacy would allow thousands to do so.

Hibernia became a park when she sold it to the county in 1963. A park where many note the changing seasons across the wooded estate. At Hibernia Park mountain-bikers race along its trails, the deeper pools of the Brandywine chill wintertime fishermen in hip boots, skiers watch the mansion frost with snow, as do those who gather at the door of the big house for a Christmastime tour of the household that was once divided over a Yuletide squabble.

On what always seems the hottest day of the year, thousands of people pull coolers and lawn chairs from their cars and migrate to the park field at Hibernia. Come the second Saturday every August the Old Fiddlers Picnic, a tradition that began sixty years ago, settles into this expanse of fieldgrass in the Brandywine's north country. The strains of the fiddlers fight and mingle along the meadow's edge. Bands of guitar and banjo, harmonica and tambourine, set the Appalachian air for the tunes they'll exchange through the grove. Even here, beneath the leafy trees, where the sun cannot belt through the dense foliage, the air is hot.

Among the old fiddlers is Snook McFalls, who lives beside the other Brandywine Creek in Downingtown. He is seventy, retired after twenty-six years as an offset pressman in the box shop of a local paper company. He is one of the best musicians in the valley, and he doesn't read music because he doesn't have to. He has a hundred or so melodies stored in his head, "regular country-western tunes" he's taught himself from Slim Long records or the radio.

As a boy, Snook scrubbed floors in the local store after school, saved enough money to buy a three-quarter size violin from a fiddler called Billy Doan, and then he started teaching himself to play. "Mom used to chase me to the attic when I was learning. When I first started," he says, "I guess I was screech, screech, screech." But it wasn't long before he was fiddling Liberty and Orange Blossom Special and the songs that were shooting out of Nashville with the starchiness and pep of a square dancer's crinoline. McFalls' band practices every Saturday night at Charlie Gable's house, and the foursome books events like the Sugar Maple Festival in the early spring, Grange picnics, and the summertime fiddlers' gathering.

Old fiddlers are growing sparse, and young ones are few and far between. Snook McFalls knows he's a passing breed. "There's not a lot of people that like to play fiddle, I guess. I don't know why. I guess it's just hard to get started. People can get their fingers working, but they can't get the bow working. That's the whole trouble," McFalls says. His face is calm, even as the bow begins darting over the strings. "It takes a lot of patience."

Snook McFalls

Warren Mercer, Master of Ceremonies, hasn't missed a year of the Old Fiddlers since the picnic began two generations ago. He came close once. He'd taken a spill on some steps the day before a picnic, hit his head, and the cut took six stitches. His doctor told him he'd better take it easy for a while, but when Mercer sat down in his chair that Saturday afternoon and tuned in the local radio station, he was like a bull in the chute. WCOJ was broadcasting the fiddlers, and it sounded so terrific that he said to his wife, "Honey, get my clothes. We're going to the picnic."

For the umpty-umpth time he steps up on the stage at Hibernia with spunk that defies his near eighty-one years as much as his alabaster smooth face. He says his thank-yous and his God-bless-yous to the crowd. Then, with that usual grin, that gentle spark in his eye that had calmed anxious children when as Santa Claus he hoisted them to his knee in the old Mosteller's Department Store in West Chester, he introduces the first set of bands. The Downhomers, Lancaster Bluegrass, and Jens and her Brandywine Friends were about to fiddle and strum some of his favorite, foot-stomping tunes, and you could feel his enthusiasm surround the crowd like a lap robe.

The group in the field is half the size that it was when the picnic first moved from a meadow in Parkesburg to an amusement park down river at Lenape. People wonder what will become of the Old Fiddlers Picnic in the coming years, when Warren Mercer relinquishes his role as emcee and the magical old fiddlers, like blind Johiah Kirkoff who died a few years back, are memories. They used to lead Kirkoff across the stage, and you had to wonder if he would be able to play at all. Then he would pull his bow across the strings and the music would leap from the bandstand with more energy than the old man's legs could ever muster. And when the crowd began to clap to Kirkoff's tune, his fingers would move with the suppleness of a spider spinning silk.

Not all of the fiddlers are old, but it is the old-timer—like Snook McFalls or Peter Kraus—who best conveys the spirit of old-time fiddling. Kraus holds his fiddle like Kirkoff did, not beneath his chin but in the crook of his elbow. "Old-timers used to hold their fiddles like this in Berks County, where I grew up," he says after leaving the stage. He is himself an old-timer now, whether he thinks so or not. A man reminded him of how he used to play at hoedowns at his father's Reading farm sixty years ago, and Kraus took off his cap as if to cool his head, put

Hibernia waterfall

Pages 88,89: Summer, Hibernia

Rock Run

it on again, and smiled a smile of remembrance.

Below Hibernia, the Brandywine chisels through the limestone toward a town called Rock Run, where houses of wood and tarpaper and stone longing for repointing grip the hillsides with their back walls. The houses seem to shrink back from the road that winds as close to their front doors as a run to a mill. Some were built when the road was a welcome neighbor. When the people could stand in the door and call out to carriages and carts that passed by to collect the news from the surrounding villages and share some news of their own.

Kurtz's Dam formed a reservoir beside Rock Run, a summer retreat with boathouses along its shore. That water is gone now, save the gentle run of the creek and the town another forgotten place along the northern edge of the Great Valley. The railroad runs beneath one arch of a high stone bridge, the Brandywine beneath another. Both industry and recreation have left Rock Run, left it sleepy and alone. And the Brandywine passes through as if it, too, has forgotten this valley in its anticipation of the big mill town just around the bend.

Coatesville. Depressed with the layoffs at the steel plant, teetering on the edge of urban renewal, but always in some way rich for its

Fishing, Coatesville

poverty and grayness. Steel forged this city, and with the rise and fall and recovery of industry, Coatesville, too, has risen and fallen.

The Brandywine Iron Works, established in 1810, became the Lukens Steel Company and transformed this small town that was then on the edge of wilderness—a town named for the son of an Irish Quaker—into an industrial giant. From atop the hill that rises above these square miles of industry, the rowhouses and streets of small shops are a colony around the mammoth black queen bee of a steel plant. The snaking Brandywine cuts through like dark nectar and the railroad tracks are tunnels to and from the cells. In the valley, in the heart of Coatesville, there is a melt shop within one of the steel plant's massive black metal buildings that is drama and war and hell. Sirens sound and men in silver jumpsuits prepare the furnace for a pour. Charged with electricity by snaking wires and glowing with sun-like intensity, three graphite heating rods melt the pre-sorted aftermath of demolition. Scraps of cars that crashed or succumbed to age become orange, liquified, like frozen beef stock over a gas range. Later they'll harden into giant ingots, then press out into neat glowing plates, cool and darken.

Lukens Steel is the 180-year old legacy of the Brandywine Iron Works, established by an iron master downstream along Buck Run. Isaac Pennock passed down his knowledge and his forges to his son-in-law Charles Lloyd Lukens, a Philadelphia physician who took on the iron trade after marrying Pennock's daughter Rebecca. Three years later, Lukens took over operation of the Coatesville mill, and soon his business—the first to roll boiler plates in America—rivaled Bethlehem and Pittsburgh. In 1825, after his death, his widow assumed the head of the ironworks, a daring move for a woman at the time. The first years were tough, and Rebecca Lukens depended on Charles Brooke, her friend and fellow iron master in Hibernia, to supply bar iron and charcoal blooms on credit to Brandywine Iron Works.

Today, Lukens flourishes in spite of a depressed steel market. It is the major provider of jobs in Coatesville. And, with the increase of mechanization in the increasingly high-tech industry, it also takes away jobs. Good has come of the changes in industry for the environment. Today's Brandywine passes below roads and through culverts and emerges from the steel plant no worse for its journey through the mill. It heads due west and south beside the railroad track to Modena, a

Lukens Steel

town literally in Coatesville's shadow.

It seems that everything Modena does is in the steeltown's shadow. Steel pushed its way west to the first stop on the Wilmington & Northern when the line conjoined Coatesville and Wilmington in 1831, intersecting the Pennsylvania Railroad out of Philadelphia. And any industry that grew here grew because of what was first wrought in Coatesville.

Luria Brothers still operates what was once one of the largest scrap metal yards in the country—reclaiming old railroad cars, separating the scrap iron and steel, and shipping salvage to the steel mills. There is a Modena foundry that makes manhole covers, a bus garage, and an oil refinery, all so subtle that you'd barely know they were there until the close of a shift, when the workers emerge from the long, flat factories.

Nestled in a crook of the shady stream-carved valley, the town has never let go its notion of power, born of industry. Like Coatesville to steel, Modena was dependent on the success of its paper mill. And with shutdowns and changes in ownership, growth eventually slowed to a halt. Perhaps it was Modena's struggle to hold its own that urged the townspeople in the 1920s to petition the County Court for borough status. Yet even to this day, Modena has only five hundred or so residents and a hundred houses.

While future growth seems less a threat to the steeply graded, rock-based town than those up and out of the valley, Modena has compiled one of the most thorough comprehensive plans for development in the county—completed in 1981, before more threatened towns had an inkling to devise one. Modena holds more surprises.

It is the smallest municipality in Chester County, and yet it has a full-time mayor. And with not even so much as a single traffic light, the town has its own fire company. Borough Hall shares the firehouse, yet more political protocol is determined at the local bar, perhaps, than at the council's monthly meetings. Alex and Jerry's, in what could best be described as the center of town, has an almost frightening gray facade. The tavern's brown-and-white metal awnings close in atop its windows like sleepy eyelids. Inside, the exterior gives way to a dim warmth where Alex, the owner, and Jerry, his wife, tap beers and swap stories.

It was another Alex—Alexander Mode—who gave this town its name. He bought a chunk of land along the Brandywine in 1736 and

Alex and Jerry's, Modena

built a sawmill in the wilderness. Mode's son converted it into a paper mill the year the iron mills were established in the tiny neighboring village of Coatesville. More than a century later the Beach and Arthur Company bought the paper mill and had enough pull to convince the townspeople to change Modena's name to Paperville in 1937. But in those days before zip codes, Paperville's mail would often end up in a Bucks County town by the name of Piperville. And so it was decided, after seven years of confusion, that the borough would reclaim the name of its founder.

Land along the Brandywine to the south of Modena is rough-hewn, dotted here and there with metal and cinder block industrial buildings amidst the trees. Places like the shop Vince Newhauser leases from the old Lipsett Brothers scrap reclamation factory. He uses the furnace that once melted down retired railroad cars to heat and bend steel rods for industry.

The garages and warehouses grow far between as the Brandywine ventures south from Coatesville's valley. Trees flood the valley, and rocky Alpine gorges, like those that follow the East Branch to Downingtown, rise above the current. The road twists between the

water and rock until it happens upon Mortonville.

White water gushes over a dam and down an expanse of stacked stone, as if racing to reach its merge with the East Branch. Below the dam the creek becomes moody—black and slow again—and passes below a stone-arch bridge to the carcass of the Mortonville Grist, Flour and Sawmill. The rock-walled white elephant of a mill has been for sale for years; its skeleton fallen beyond simple restoration, with the road to Parkesburg pushed forcefully against its northern wall.

Down Strasburg Road, along the route drovers once traveled to Philadelphia, Wayne and Janet Sammons stood in a dewy field on their farm where they had raised wheat and corn and children. On the morning they auctioned off the farm equipment, strangers' children ran beside the spring-tooth harrow and corn wagon, the farm machinery looking suspiciously like playground equipment. The childrens' parents were busy eyeing the dew-coated machines, and drawing mental lines above top dollar they would silently nod past as the bidding moved through the field. It was the week before Easter and an auctioneer's gibberish decorated the April air like fancy piping on a sugar egg.

The farm would see more activity that day than ever before. Cars and trucks climbed the dirt road behind the house and venders lured bidders from the auction wagon with hotdogs and pretzels. The auctioneer's assistant held up a bucket of golf balls. "What do I hear?" he began. "Do I hear two dollars?"

"It just goes to show," Sammons says above the caller's voice, "You never throw nothing away 'cause somebody else will always want it."

He is smiling, but he knows that we know he is sorry. "When you work real hard at something, it's hard to see it go," Mrs. Sammons says. Her husband is climbing up the rise to talk to a man eyeing his gleaming green and yellow tractor.

"I'm going to lease this land to a nursery operation. You can't make a living with a small farm any more," he says. Sammons began by selling twenty head of Angus in early spring, and finally, the harrows, mowers, corn planter, picker, wagon, elevator, haybine, sprayer, and lime spreader spanned the hilltop. The machines were his tie to the land. As bidders carted the last piece away, only the grass was his. And the soil, newly turned, would soon be planted not with crops but with merchandise.

Buck Run spills into the Brandywine not far from the Sammons'

Page 96: Mortonville Dam   *Pages 98,99: Fog, Brandywine Creek Road* farm. This, the most important tributary upon the entire length of this river, is newly nourished from its convergence with its sister creek, a pretty flow called Doe Run. It is as wide as the Brandywine it feeds, and it once supported eight mills of its own. As their stones succumbed to the passing of cold winters and hard rains, those nineteenth-century mills have long since been whittled to stubs. A ruin alongside Don Silknitter's house is the ghost of Isaac Pennock's 1799 Federal Slitting Mill of the Rokeby Iron Works—the mill that inspired Pennock to found the Brandywine works in Coatesville. A hundred feet from the fallen Rokeby wall, a bright new mill perches over the drop of the oldest dam in the valley.

Don Silknitter manufactures electricity here. His power plant looks from the roadside more like a child's playhouse, its blue clapboard frame perched over the drop, curtains in the windows, a white iron garden bench on the front porch. Inside, the mill house is all business. Turbines beneath the floor turn steadily with the falling water, and for that Silknitter doesn't intend to write another check to the power company. As the public utility is legally bound to purchase back the power he and his neighbors don't use, he will, in fact, receive checks from Philadelphia Electric.

After Don and his wife Joan bought their old white house on the site of the slitting mill, beside the healthy run on its way to meet the Brandywine, they began to cut through three years of red tape that stood between their potentially powerful dam and the utility. Between trips to Harrisburg, Don and his brother Ron, a professional engineer, dug the 100-year-old turbine out from its 43-year hibernation in silt.

The turbines are like those that replaced waterwheels 150 years ago. The French first recognized that a flow of water through a pipe and into the tanks would extract maximum power from moving water. That the water would hit the entire surface of a turbine with greater force than the buckets on a wooden wheel. Silknitter's tanks are custom designed, the generators military surplus from aircraft landing gear. Together the homespun works light his and his neighbors' houses along the stream, while Don is teaching history at the local high school.

Below Silknitter's Mill, the twin tributaries of Buck and Doe Run drain some of the richest valley land in the east to feed the Brandywine's current. The soil is probably no more fertile than the Amish farmers' fields along the northern headwaters, but it is prettier, more sophisticated. As if draped in green silks and velvet as opposed to burlap. The hills glide well-groomed to the lowlands, the end-product of meticulous grass improvement and soil analysis. Phosphorous-rich lime was taken from the kilns that are as ruins now on the hillside, and spread thick beneath the soil across these fields.

This has traditionally been a land of cash crops—corn, soybeans, tobacco, and small grain. Hedgerows trim the fields, forming leafy borders between pastures. The brush offers protective cover for birds, for small game, and red foxes. Fields of red clover swell in summer with the haze of flies and bees, the scurry of butterflies. An eastern meadow-lark provides song from atop a fence post, while a crow stabs at a grasshopper tangled in the grass.

This is horse country. A land of gentlemen's farms, of steeplechases, fox hunts, and private polo fields. And, almost as if thrown in as a counterbalance, it is a land of horned beef steers and cowboys. Chuck and Rusty ride their ranch ponies along the fence lines to watch a herd whose lineage begins some 1800 miles southwest of Unionville.

The distinctively dark-red cows came to the valley in the late forties, when a landholder named Lammot du Pont sold the Buck and Doe Run Valley Farms to Robert Kleberg, Jr., the president and manager of the Texas-based King Ranch. Shortly after World War I, the rancher had crossbred Brahmans (a Texas-bred derivative of the so-called sacred cows of India) with Shorthorns. Kleberg named the three-quarter ton bulls Santa Gertrudis, for the original grant of land from the Crown of Spain on which his ranch was founded in 1852. His purchase of this Pennsylvania acreage was an effort to lessen the shrinkage factor—the weight loss his cattle sustained when packed into trucks and vented traincars and shipped to market over long distances. King Ranch and its western ways received a warm eastern welcome from the local people, particularly W. Plunket Stewart, Master of the Cheshire Hounds, who feared the sale of the land would destroy fox hunting property.

A red flag went up again in the late seventies. The ranch owners had decided to sell King Ranch. By this time, Chester County was growing quickly and the land was a developer's dream. The Brandy-wine Conservancy, a group formed to protect land and water resources downriver from development, joined with a limited partnership called

Doe Run cowboys

Hay truck

Buck and Doe Associates to divide the rolling pasture into large parcels. The houses in Buck and Doe valley are few and far between, and the land is securely restricted against further development.

Among the Conservancy's holdings in the valley is the Laurels—a sprawling wooded dale accessible only by a hard earthen trail that winds beside the merging of Doe Run and Buck Run. Above, there are caves with floors worn smooth by nesting animals, and subtle streams that skip down the overgrown hillside on terraced falls. Mountain laurel and rhododendron dapple the forest floor like shadow beneath the oak and maple. They climb up over the ridge, their waxy leaves a bluish silver in the scattered sunlight. Unlike the showy apple and cherry, they bloom delicate and unseen deep within the woods. They prefer to take their bed in the muted light of these taller trees. White stars and long lavender trumpets dot the twisted branches between the leaves—they bloom not as harbingers of spring like the dogwood and plum, but as reassurance in later spring that warmth and sun will penetrate even the dense thicket and summer will soon inflate the valley with its hazy air.

Where the roads have grown over just above the fork of Buck Run

Pond, Buck and Doe valley

Bridge over Doe Run

and Doe Run, twin covered bridges cross the twin creeks. One bridge is sturdy for its years, like a well-built barn, another recently rebuilt after fire and sealed off to prevent the cattle that graze in the secluded fields beyond from slipping through the wooden tunnel.

All is quiet except for a bellowing cow, an occasional screech whistle cry from a redtailed hawk or the crackle of dry leaves as a twelvepoint buck scurries up the high ridge that casts a shadow across the creek. It is hard to imagine that there was once a community strewn through this valley, that the scattered houses that remain without a thoroughfare to connect them to the civilized world were ever a part of a town.

At the first bend in the path through the Laurels, a stone house people call Angel House is being restored. It sits on a rise overlooking Doe Run; below it, steep rocks lead down to the water's edge. Plates of rock form caves down the earthen road. They are called McCorkle's Rocks.

Local legend has it that a horse thief named McCorkle lived in the house here at the time of the American Revolution. After raiding farms near and far, the outlaw would hide the horses in this quiet valley until he could sell them to either the American Army or the British soldiers. The unprincipled horse thief eventually contracted smallpox, his wife deserted him, and old McCorkle died, alone, in his house on the rocky ledge.

The crumbled foundations of a forge are not far down from Buck Run's meeting with the Brandywine. This was the furnace that Samuel, William and Jesse Laverty built in 1793 to stamp out nails and horseshoes. Hugh Steel took over the nail works in 1840 and in twenty years made the factory amongst the most efficient and profitable iron mills in the nation. It is said that the forges cast iron plates for the U.S.S. Monitor and other early battleships when the government commandeered Steel's mill at the onset of the Civil War and ran it as a munitions plant.

After the Civil War, the government returned the Laurel mill to Steel and he continued to forge gas pipes and boilers for steamships. When the orders were high, the forges glowed night and day. Then they stood idle for weeks at a time until, on February 2, 1889, the *Coatesville Weekly Times* publicized a brief news item: "Laurel Iron Works shut down on Wednesday evening. It is thought, however, the stoppage will only be for a few days." The stoppage was permanent, the plant never ran iron again, and its walls have long since tumbled alongside the creek.

Robert E. Lee lives near the old mill site on Laurel Road, a quiet stretch northeast of The Laurels. His house is separated from the Brandywine's upper bank by about an acre's-width of grassy field, its shoulder edged with the Reading Railroad track like a fading pinstripe. Lee was not born of the South, as his name would suggest, but fifteen miles upstream in West Brandywine township. He and his wife Alice have lived fifty-five years on this farm—once 130 acres, now down to 32. He used to load his milk onto train cars headed south along the Brandywine toward Wilmington.

"I remember when Bob took a sugar bag full of fifty-cent pieces and bought a horse for fifty dollars," Alice Lee says. "Things used to be simpler then." Those were the days, he chimed in, when you could take your corn to the mill in the next town to have it ground for feed. The days the creek flowed red, blue, or black, depending on the ink they were using at the paper mill up stream in Modena that afternoon. Those were the days.

Lee's barn has been a local landmark since it nearly collapsed in the blizzard of '58, the solid beams buckled under the strain and the

Mr. and Mrs. Robert E. Lee

Embreeville Mill

roofline bowed groundward like a swayback mare. He lost his hay. But he was fortunate, as some of his neighbors lost buildings and livestock. The farmers in the valley called it a "blue snow"—four feet deep and heavy—but Lee's contorted barn held that spring, and for thirty years it has teased gravity with its menacing stance.

The village of Embreeville, population somewhere in the vicinity of 60, first spread out along the Brandywine when a corn mill began to grind meal and feed there in the middle-eighteenth century. The Embree family fled France, where they had been persecuted as Huguenots. John Embree was one of over a quarter of a million Protestants to flee to England, Holland and America under the Catholic monarchy of Louis XIV. He settled in Nantmeal in the 1700s, and James Embree, a descendant, would later move south to West Bradford. Both had married Quaker women whose flight from religious persecution was not unlike their own, and the collective family became confirmed and active Quakers at the Bradford Meeting.

Two of James Embree's sons were brewers in Cincinnati, and another was a steamboat captain on the Mississippi while Mark Twain was a pilot. But a third son, William, opted for a quieter life, stayed close to home, and settled a small village around his mill. Industrious, but never exceedingly wealthy, he set up shop as brewer and storekeeper, was the first postmaster in 1830, and later served as treasurer of Chester County.

Embreeville's corn mill had been the first of the mills built along the western branch of the river. The town's grain mill would be the last to grind feed. Standing three wooden floors high atop its 200-year-old foundation, it squeezes firmly between the road and an active but non-productive millrace. For more than a century the Embreeville Mill avoided explosion and fire despite ever-present grain and flour dust that is nearly as combustible as gunpowder. Rising water was the miller's nemesis.

The race quit turning the wheel while silt was dug from the water works in the aftermath of the floods of 1855, 1885, and 1907. Giant turbines replaced the mill's water wheel in the late 1880s. They turned the cogs, turned the belts, turned more cogs, pushing the grain harvested from local farmers' fields through the works, down the chutes, down into bins and bags. The grain moved through the

Mill works, Embreeville

creaking mill until Hurricane Agnes halted its two turbines in 1972. They haven't run since.

Wilson Reynolds, the owner of the old place, dreams of hearing the cogs and belts work the bins again. He runs a grain retail business here. There are plenty of customers, but on weekends you'll find some who stop are more interested in talking about the mill than purchasing feed. A solid chestnut beam, forty-two feet long, runs the length of the first floor ceiling, and on the floor above, the grinding stones, wooden chutes that carried grain from bins to sifters and sorters, and the wooden augers, stand as they did the day the mill shut down. The chugging grind of the wheels and belts, the smell of fresh-ground grain, the powder in the air, linger ghost-like in the dim light of the lofts.

The Wilmington and Northern Railroad laid tracks along the Brandywine in 1869, and put in a station called Embreeville three-quarters of a mile from the actual village. The village that sprang up around the stop was called New Embreeville. From there the Brandywine cuts a giant horseshoe through the earth. It pushes up toward the Star-Gazer's Stone, which, until not long ago, was obscured by field flowers and tall weeds.

You wouldn't have known the small point of rock was crouching there, planted firmly in the earth, if it weren't for the blue and yellow plaque the Pennsylvania Historical and Museum Commission mounted on a pole beside the road. The sign commemorates a pair of English surveyors and their astronomical observation that in 1764 determined an accurate boundary between Maryland and Pennsylvania. Because of Charles Mason and Jeremiah Dixon, this landmark in Newlin Township would help clearly divide slave states from the free a hundred years later.

Surveying was crude before the states united. It sometimes took twenty years to determine the acreage of a large manor, no less the exact boundaries between the commonwealths. The Maryland and Pennsylvania border had been in doubt for nearly a century, and Lord Baltimore's original grant, if maintained, would have put Philadelphia and its harbor outside of William Penn's jurisdiction. Since no one knew for certain where the 40th parallel was that determined the exact boundary, Penn was granted the half of the Delmarva Peninsula between Delaware Bay and the Chesapeake that lay east of a line drawn from the latitude of Cape Henlopen. That line continued north until it met the arc of a circle drawn with a twelve-mile radius from New Castle. But who really owned what?

The states awaited a clear decision from the British courts, and finally, in 1750, Lord Hardwick decreed to maintain an original agreement—to run a line west, dividing Pennsylvania from Maryland from a point on the north-south Peninsula line, fifteen miles south of the southernmost latitude of Philadelphia. That left an 800-acre wedge between the northern arc of Delaware and the north-south line, which was later awarded to Delaware.

Mason and Dixon determined the exact location and latitude of the Philadelphia point before moving west to Chester County to set up shop for final observations. After they had determined the exact astronomical location of the stone, they began to cut a "visto" about 25 feet wide through woods and brush. They thought the Star-Gazer's Stone was placed at a most convenient spot—between the two branches of the Brandywine to save the crossing of rivers—but it wasn't long before they found that they had to cross the meandering Brandywine three times on their southern extension. The two followed

Zeke Hubbard, Northbrook

their line fifteen miles south, and established with great accuracy a corner from which the famous east-and-west boundary line could be run. They carried the border line some 230 miles west until hostile Indians were said to have turned them back. The Royal Society took advantage of Mason and Dixon's calculations to measure for the first time the exact length of a degree of latitude on land, a distance of 68.826 miles.

So that is the Star-Gazer's Stone. Nothing spectacular to look at by any means, but meaningful for its place in history. It doesn't stand alone in the field any longer because the field was surveyed again, this time for development, in the spring of 1988. The weeds and wildflowers were bulldozed and a house built beside the stone, plot lines in place.

A string of old houses hugs the Strasburg Road half a mile north of the West Branch, and just west of the East. A friends meeting, an inn, a church and a firehall, together a small strip of a town called Marshallton. The Marshalton Inn looks much as it did when the drovers stopped in from the old road to Lancaster. The inn sponsors a triathlon every year—a bike race south to the West Branch Brandywine at Northbrook, where competitors slide canoes into the cold water and paddle in pairs to the bridge at Wawaset. From there, a foot race back to the field beside the canoe launch, where they pick up their bikes and race to the finish beside the starting line.

Northbrook Canoe Company is the most popular launch along the creek. Canoes fill the barns and sheds, perch on racks, are piled high behind old troopers of trucks. On a busy summer day, Zeke Hubbard launches sixty canoeists, many of them first-time paddlers, into the Brandywine. Buses head south to bring them back to the launch, back with new knowledge of the river habitat.

As the paddles lap the water with a pacifying rhythm, the view of the creek from the canoe thwart is unlike any a road or bridge could offer. Sentinel painted turtles sun themselves on logs and rocks, with heads held high as if to guard their sporadic perches. As the canoe slices through their creek, you can be sure that each turtle will push out his withered feet and slip down below the water. There is a different rhythm along the river habitat. It moves at the water's pace. A great blue heron lifts off, disturbed, from a shallow pool, his spindly legs stretched out in tow. In flight he follows the water line as if it were a road. There are dilapidated cabins and dream homes on stilts along the banks, weekend anglers, and other canoeists.

Below Northbrook the creek branches into channels to form islands; it passes the site of Trimble's Ford, where British soldiers first crossed the Brandywine to surprise the rebels awaiting confrontation downstream at Chadds Ford. Colonel Hannum and Squire Cheyney rode off from there to inform an incredulous George Washington that his flank was endangered. Both men were members of the Bradford Meeting, as was Humphry Marshall, who built a sawmill and gristmill near Trimble's Ford and a beautiful stone house in the town which took his name.

Marshall was best known as a botanist. His *Arbustum Americanum* (1785), the first American botanical essay, was inspired along the banks of the Brandywine. His own forest of ornamental trees was the second arboretum in America, the first created near Philadelphia by Marshall's cousin, John Bartram.

Before the Revolution, Northbrook was another of the productive, peaceful Indian villages that spread along the Brandywine. The Indians were at first fascinated by the ways of Penn's brood. During the first years, the white men traveled their trails and battled the winters in inappropriate dress and makeshift shelters. And were it not for the natives, many of those Quaker families who had ventured across the ocean in search of a better life may not have survived the raw wilderness. But soon the white man had wrapped himself in European finery and trappings and built solid houses of gneiss that soon weathered to a soft orange shade not far from that of the wigwam villages. The settlers prospered on the rich farmland with running water. They built mills to process the maize the Indians had shared and the grains they had cultivated from their native lands across the sea.

Further south along the Brandywine the Swedes had settled, and with them they brought disease from Europe, strong drink, and civilization that would shrink the Indians' hunting grounds near the Delaware Bay. While most natives preferred not to change their lives, others were snared by the richness of it all, the fineness of the white man's pipes, the warm numbing of his alcohol, the opulence of his simple glass beads. They were not forcefully chased from the land, but squeezed out by the settlers who, not unlike some developers today, enticed them to trade their homeland for goods that would fade and rust.

Indian Rock perches above the creek not far from the Northbrook Bridge. While geologically insignificant, it marks the southern bounds of the Lenni-Lenape's last hold on the Brandywine. In 1705, twenty-two years after William Penn had purchased the land of present-day Wilmington, the Delaware chiefs insisted that the Quaker had deeded them a mile on each side of the entire river save the East Branch. They claimed the Brandywine hunting and fishing lands beginning at the river's mouth, and turning off at the merge to follow the West Branch to its spring-fed source in the Welsh Hills. But without documentation the Indians had no success pressing their claim.

To make amends, Penn officially purchased from the Indians, in 1706, a two-mile-wide strip from the mouth of the Brandywine to this bankside stone we now call Indian Rock. The Lenni-Lenape retained their own two-mile-wide strip from there to the source of the Brandywine. The linear holding, a mile on either side of the northern creek, was to belong to the band of Delaware Indians until their third generation had grown old and blind. A rather obscure agreement, and the last remaining Indians, who called themselves "Freemen," would leave their small wigwam villages here beside the West Branch before that time. They had been denied a peaceful land to hunt and fish. They felt the land belonged to no one, that it was to be shared for its bounty, and this portion could not appease their loss.

There wasn't the kind of conflict in the Brandywine Valley between the natives and colonists that occurred to the south and north, yet some Indians lived in fear that they would be mistaken for warlike tribes and put to death. Masses of Lenape Indians moved voluntarily from their Brandywine camps shortly after the French and Indian War. Most journeyed northwest to the Wyoming Valley or to Mercer County near Pennsylvania's border with Ohio. Flight was inevitable as elements of economy replaced barter; the Lenni-Lenape were not a tribe even to exchange wampum. Westward expansion eventually pushed them across the American frontier to Oklahoma, where their descendants now live. They do not occupy a reservation, but are United States citizens and part of the state's general population.

Intermarriage with whites and more than a century of cross-culturization have erased native customs, and only a handful of the children of the lost Lenape nation can speak their native tongue. All that remains of them on their ancestral lands are the overgrown outlines of their trails along the creek, some legends, and the names their presence gave the villages here.

In a small log house, off a wooded road a mile or so west of Northbrook, Indian Hannah made brooms and concocted her medicines. In the dim light she wove ash and oak splints tightly to baskets. The berries of the forest gave her a palette of red, orange, green, and purple dyes that would stain her dark fingers as she smoothed across the weave. She was a Freeman, the last of the Lenni-Lenape tribe to remain on her native land. Hannah's house stood not far from one of the tribe's burial grounds.

She would sometimes pass that sacred place as she walked from town to town, her dogs Elmun and Putmoe at the hem of her skirts, to sell her wares. The dogs would lie at her feet as she read fortunes in the homes of villagers, those who wished to know what her prophecy might bring. As the years passed, families would take her in and share food and clothing. But her home in old age was the county home, more accurately the poorhouse. She died there in 1802, at the age of seventy-one, and she was buried nearby.

People memorialize her, perhaps because she was the last of a tribal nation. But the stories that remain of her life along the creek reveal a woman who would be remembered regardless of her race. Indian Hannah felt that the land was rightfully hers and her people's. She disregarded "No Trespassing" signs, fences, gates or stone walls that separated property. She felt mill dams should not block running streams, but beaver dams should not be pillaged. While her ancestors had cleared the forest floor for hunting, she argued strongly that shrubs, where small birds take shelter, should not be burnt and raked away.

In the old Grange hall in Northbrook, not far from the woods where Indian Hannah's cabin stood, Honey Johnson (a member of the Marshallton Grange for fifty-one years) was slicing peaches by the bushel. She was chatting with her friend Catherine Trimble in the kitchen. The Grange had bought dozens of the bulbous fruits from the Barnards' orchard up the road. Healthy peaches, no worse for the wear of the early summer drought. A good thing, since the Peach Festival has been on the Grange's calendar come rain or shine the second Thursday in August since 1950.

A bingo caller's voice resonated from the other room as players scanned the paper cards that framed long folding tables. The players were trying their luck at prizes stacked at the front of the room—a bag of sugar, an ice chest, a fancy shoe horn. The Grange has to buy a permit for the bingo, and that gets kind of expensive, so they hold it just once a year, at the Peach Festival. Behind the hall, five plastic milk bottles were set neatly atop cement blocks, only to be hit down again by a softball-wielding child. Three throws for a dollar. Balloons were popping from the steady throw of a dart, and a small boy slid down a cellar door. Harry Perdue was manning the lottery—a quarter Angus at a dollar a ticket. Drawing at 11 p.m.

Paul Roberts loaded his haywagon full of families and pulled them behind his John Deere, up around the cars parked in the field and back to the path beside the Grange hall. When the light faded to a deep gray, he turned on his spot beam and navigated the tractor through the darkness. A child yelled, "Mr. Roberts, can you take us through the woods?" and he let out a quick, hardy laugh.

Mature fruit trees line the roads south of Northbrook and stretch over the hills. The valley is well suited to apples. In spring the branches are ethereal in white blossom, and come fall they are covered in deep green leaf as the trees around them paint the landscape orange, yellow, red. After the first frost halts the growing season in October, the harvest begins. The trees are too busy in autumn to change the color of their leaves. Their branches stay green as they bend groundward with the weight of hundreds of ripe red apples.

Of all seasons, autumn looks best upon the Brandywine Valley. It cloaks the hills and forests in the colors of the farmhouses, the lodens and tans. Northern winds bring crisp Canadian air to clear the haze and stillness of dead September better than a summer rain ever could. Geese, too, travel south with the wind. First their approaching honks, and then the familiar, collective black angle in the sky signal autumn before the colors change across the hills. Orchard workers fill crates the size of bathtubs with the prime apples beginning in October below Northbrook. Then they gather the windfalls that will go into the cider press. On brisk autumn weekends, the potential piebakers arrive. They walk between the rows of golden and deep red fruits as if browsing, pluck, and drop the apples into buckets.

One orchard-keeper, Richard Barnard, is a seventh-generation descendant of a Quaker family that came from England to clear these

Apples, Barnard's orchard

Chester County fields for farming. His grandfather built the white stuccoed house that snuggles into the apple grove in 1862 for $2,700, and he was the first to plant rows of apple trees along these hills. The early orchardmen knew that this is a prime spot for apples. The gentle slopes encourage the cooler air to settle below, so that the trees hold their harvest above the frost line until the picking is done.

Once there were orchards throughout these valleys. There are only five or so today, and it is the local buyer, not the large distributor, who keeps the Barnards in business. Richard Barnard and his son Louis sell most of their harvest of MaCoun, Jonathan, Red and Yellow Delicious from their thirty-five acres locally. "You don't get rich at it," the father says of the business that his son will carry on. "There's a lot of development pressure, but we're going to hang on. You've just gotta love it."

Down the road from the Barnard farm, past the neighboring Northbrook Orchards, is an old house; across the road a barn with the

Winter

Albertson barn, Marshallton

fat stone supports so common to this valley. This was Horatio Myrick's homestead. The farmer loved this valley and willed his 200-acre property to the Brandywine Valley Association in 1981. The association began in the early forties, when a few men began mailing out flyers, asking some questions of residents alongside the Brandywine.

They asked, "Do you have washouts or erosion? Does your well run dry? Are you bothered by pollution upstream? Does your farmland yield crops as large as those of five or ten years ago? Can you get all the help you need on soil erosion problems?" And in the tradition of the pamphleteers, the men garnered wide response. Answers began flooding in, meetings were organized to address the concerns. The group's founders—Clayton M. Hoff, Environmentalist; Robert G. Struble, Specialist in Agriculture; and J. Howard Mendenhall, Forester—set up offices in Wilmington and West Chester. The first small watershed organization in America was formed.

The Brandywine Valley Association (BVA) sought to educate farmers who had neglected to take measures against soil erosion. To help them level the land so that the water would descend smoothly toward the banks rather than plunging into the water with fresh-plowed topsoil. They pushed to have declared a Soil Conservation District for Chester County and enlisting the support of the U.S. Geological Survey operated flow gauging, rain gauging, and silt-sampling stations. The BVA has since worked with government agencies and industry to protect water, land, and air in the 330-square-mile watershed. It has encouraged factories and homeowners to lessen run-off of raw sewage and waste that were killing Brandywine fish and waterfowl. Today the valley's dominant threats are population growth, the leveling of the land, and the continuous sloughing of silt into the creek and its tributaries.

Bob Struble, Jr., the son of the man who helped to found the BVA and for whom the Struble Lake and Trail were named, sits at the director's desk at the BVA headquarters on the old Myrick farm. He is continuing his father's struggle to preserve and maintain the Brandywine and its surrounding soil, forests, wildlife, and recreation areas. The Brandywine Valley Association is more than a watchdog for the creek. It is an education center, where children and adults learn Indian lore and such things as how to identify the hollow a deer makes in the weeds when she beds down, and the difference between an arrow-wood and a red osier dogwood.

With the founding of the H.E. Myrick Conservation Center, the fields and woods the farmer once roamed became nature trails. You might hear a horned owl in the woods nearby, or the cries of a red-tailed hawk as he rides the thermal layer on four feet of outspread wings, eyeing the fields for toads and snakes, rabbits, and wily weasels. Myrick's springhouse stoops beside a gargantuan oak. When the October winds begin to blow, Boy Scouts transform the barn where he raised cattle across the road into a haunted house.

A small village called Wawaset, its name derived perhaps from a Lenni-Lenape word meaning "the settling place of the wild geese," is the final settlement alongside the West Branch. The geese still come here. Dropping down from the sky with wings outspread they skid awkwardly, feet first, into the water. They are on their flyway between Canada and the Chesapeake Bay, the same journey their ancestors took when passing the Indian encampment here two centuries ago. Barely a cluster of houses today, the village was first called Seeds Ford for Emmor Seeds, a local farmer who was born the year the Revolution was fought on the banks below. It was renamed when the Wilmington and Northern laid its rails. Like so many other villages along the train's path, it took the name of the station built beside the creek. The West Branch flows wide beneath a concrete span that replaced an earlier concrete bridge, that replaced what was once Seed's Bridge, the longest covered wooden bridge in Chester County.

Just below the bridge, the water deepens and meets the East Creek. The branches, just before they flow together to form a near-perfect Y, are like identical twins with opposite personalities. Toughened by its run through the steel mill in Coatesville and across more rugged land, teeming and boisterous, the West Branch charges into the merge. You can hear it trip over rocks in its enthusiasm, and after a heavy rain its water stirs up a little muddier than the East Branch. The East merely drifts toward the union with slight apprehension, silent and composed.

The land that began at the lower sandstone slopes of Welsh Mountain and has separated these creeks through the Great Valley's limestone, looks from here like nothing so much as one of the islands downstream. The patch of earth that divides the branches ends in a subtle point, jutting into the convergence where shad once fought the current to choose a northward path toward spawning ground.

T H E   M E R G E

There is a subtle richness about this lower Brandywine. It has neither great breadth nor tremendous flow, but many people have channeled their ideas into its current and in so doing have brought about change and progress.

The river crosses a state border here, and edges past the remains of small grist, paper and textile mills to the massive workings of industry. From the time the first Swedish settlers set foot beside the river's end, the water has provided the means for ingenuity and progress. In the wake of two centuries of industry that have both augmented and partially destroyed the richness of this land, some people now seek to return nature's blessing. They have worked to overcome the harm that has been wrought, and to preserve or replenish what remains.

There is a reunion of sorts at the confluence of the East and West Branches. It is a reunion of waters that first spilled through the earth to form headwater creeks and then parted to pass through distant meadows and separate towns. The short path from Shaw's Bridge ends where the land that divides the twin creeks drops beneath the water. Flat meadow rims the east bank. On the high and jagged western ridge a stand of pines, silhouetted, forms a stockade against the setting sun. Near the water line, railroad ties are heaped alongside the old Wilmington and Northern tracks. The merge is an empty place.

Some say the creeks become a river here, and yet others insist that the single flow should be called Brandywine Creek. The Brandywine Conservancy, which holds office downstream, dubs it the Brandywine River. The Brandywine Valley Association contends that it is a creek. Even governmental bureaucracy is of little help in settling the dispute; while the U.S. Geological Survey labels its maps Brandywine Creek, the Army Corps of Engineers calls it the Brandywine River. It pales in comparison to other American rivers in terms of width and depth, flow and temperament. Ask a Mississippian what he thinks, and the Brandywine will be deemed a trickle. Yet meet a New Englander, accustomed to crossing culverts labeled Such-and-Such River, and he'll surely tell you this is a full-fledged river.

Oddly enough, in Delaware, where the waterway will have swelled to more of a river's proportions with a channel depth of twenty feet near its mouth, the old-timer will bellow, "The Brandywine ain't no river. It's a crick." The singular flow will widen and contract, widen and contract again, as it journeys south. Past sturdy stone houses and farms toward the forests above the city of Wilmington. And then industry will line up along its closing banks to crowd the Brandywine's finish line like grandstands at a racetrack.

A destination for many canoeists from the north, the left bank of the closing East Branch is worn smooth as potter's clay from the hulls of boats. The slick bank also launches others on a different journey toward wide water where willows and sycamores flip lanky roots, like drinking straws, to the water's edge. After the merge, the water's confidence seems bolstered by its sudden growth spurt. It drops purposefully, then the broader current slows and the flow is held in check by two dams. First a smaller dam, holding the natural race that edges around the eastern side of an island. A heap of stone pushes back the water. The Lenape Dam once harnessed the current to power a large cotton factory.

Today the stones provide rafters and canoeists fleeting white water should they decide not to portage. On hot Saturday afternoons, the paddles of passing canoes splash steadily through the deeper water. As the paddlers give their arms a rest beyond the dam, the long shells drift lazily beneath the rumble of slow traffic across the Route 52 bridge at Lenape.

Unlike most of the other roadway crossings that afford only a fleeting glimpse of the water, if any view at all, Lenape's is a looking bridge. Come winter, wooden tables hibernate beneath company picnic pavilions at Brandywine Park. Ducks line the banks before the long brick Lenape Inn, a restaurant wide with windows turned upon the slow water.

Thousand-ton forging presses in a factory beside the inn stamp out parts used in steam generation, ball valves for nuclear generating stations, forgings for coal- and oil-fired power plants. Lenape Forge, with additions upon additions, was once a trolly hangar. After a local farmer sold sixteen acres to the president of West Chester Street Railway Company, it marked the end of the line.

And with the streetcar, an amusement park grew from the meadow across the river. The rides of Lenape Park once spun and sped where the Brandywine Picnic Park now covers the land. It was the sort of place where families proudly drove their first motor cars, where they stored rowboats and canoes along the banks for weekend outings. For seventy-five years, long after the trolley stopped running and the rails were taken up or covered over, laughter and screams darted out across the water from atop the lattice-supported track of a roller coaster. Accompanied by the drum beat and calliope song of the carousel, boys would vie for the brass ring while astride their mounts. First they would scramble for the deer, and from his rising back they could grab that ring, proudly but quickly thread it over his antler, and gear up for the next go-around, and a chance at another free ride.

When the park closed in the early seventies, the carousel was dismantled and its herd of animals sold as ornaments to scattered buyers. The huddle of houses above the park, once closed tight as the carousel come winter and aired out again in late spring, are year-round dwellings now. Across the river, artist Tom Bostelle paints shadows in the Aeolian Palace, the old pavilion where couples once danced the night away or watched the moonlit river slip past the porch in the deepening shadows of night. The artist's friend Tanya Boucher is a sculptor. She shapes forms in her studio, the old refreshment stand that flanks the dance hall.

For centuries, even before the Quakers settled along the river, this broad water and grassy plain was a favorite gathering spot in summer. The Lenni-Lenape who inspired the village's name, had reluctantly but peacefully shared these fertile waters with other tribes who came to pull from vine-woven dragnets eels and shad easily trapped here on their journey to spawning grounds. The Indians here were also farmers. They planted rows of corn nearby, or maize as they called it, good eating when steamed in the husk or dried and then pounded to meal with mortar and pestle for pone.

The tribes purposefully moved, season by season, to different camps alongside the creek they called Wawasan. Guided by the spawning shad or the calendar for planting and harvest, they established narrow trails that would become trading paths and then roads along the Wawasan's edge. Those trails connecting Indian villages later spanned quiet Quaker settlements. Then industry took hold, tracks were laid, and the small towns became railroad flag stops. Cossart,

Power lines

Pocopson cow

Chadds Ford Junction, Pocopson, Brandywine Park, Lenape, and Wawaset at the forks. The Laurel Iron Works and Lukens Steel in Coatesville inspired the Wilmington and Reading Railroad's path on up alongside the river's West Branch: Northbrook, Glenhall, Embreeville, Laurel, Mortonville, and Modena.

Surveys for a freight line connecting industrial Reading with Wilmington began the year the Civil War ended—when investors hoped to carve out a piece of the lucrative rail market then dominated by Philadelphia. In 1869 the cars began coursing through the valley—some hauling freight, others passengers—until financial crisis had a disastrous effect on the railroad in 1873. Investors' bonds, when called two years later, were worth nothing, and the railroad was sold the next year. The line was reorganized on New Yea's Day 1877 as the Wilmington and Northern Railroad—to survive the coming years of hardship—and freight trains continue to move along its tracks today.

During the 1870s, during the initial glory of the rails, a Pocopson township farmer named Frank Graff prettied up a public picnic ground across his grove of white oaks along the Brandywine a half mile below Lenape. Birmingham Park was another of those attractions that sprang up in the Victorian age wherever a few good natural resources and human resourcefulness coincided. Figuring the shiny new rails could carry day trippers by the carload to his stop below Route 926, the farmer stretched a footbridge across the Brandywine, opposite where Pocopson Run joins the river.

Mr. Graff figured right. The passenger trains followed the Brandywine's curves to the park from Wilmington, Reading, and Coatesville, sometimes bringing more than a thousand people to the broad water's banks. There they would disembark with their picnic baskets and cross the footbridge to the eastern bank. Tennis courts, baseball and cricket fields, filled the flat land beside the Brandywine. There was a dance pavilion that glowed on into the Gay Nineties. The water itself provided bathing and good fishing, and the captain of a tiny excursion boat called the "Minnehaha," would fire up the steam engine, collect ten cents from his passengers as they boarded her deck, and direct his craft on a brief cruise upstream.

The Birmingham Park footbridge was taken up each winter to keep it from washing out during spring floods. When the creek iced over, all was quiet save the raw cut of skates on the frozen water. Brandywine Park Station closed in 1895, the year Lenape Park opened upstream, and it wasn't long before Graff's meadow returned to pastureland.

The excursion boat, the need to pull the footbridge come winter, the monumental fordings on this creek, all seem disproportionate to what today seems a meager flow. George Fox, the founder and leader of the Society of Friends, once passed through the Brandywine Valley and later said that the Brandywine was "a desperate river, which had in it many rocks, and broad stones, very hazardous to us and our horses." The Brandywine today—even in the floods of spring—is a remnant of its former self, the gentler flow the result of conscious taming upstream.

The water deepens south of Lenape and Pocopson. Occasionally it breaks loose through grassy plains, widens and spills over into lily-webbed marshes, but then straightens again to the rigors of its banks in a neat descent. The river's consistent drop, along with its location on the frontier of the developing nation, made it among the most productive of working waterways. Far more productive in terms of milling than the larger rivers that surround it. The Brandywine once was so replete with water wheels that it was called "The Creek of a Hundred Mills."

Tributaries, too, formed natural races. Mills fed on the current of Plum Run and Radley Run from the east, Pocopson Creek from the west, and Bennett's Run and Brinton Run, Ring and Harvey Run downstream.

The tiny village of Chadds Ford grew along the river's path nearly a century before the Revolution. Initially it was a Quaker milling and farming village, born of the Brinton and Gilpin families, the Taylors and Rings, and a shoemaker named Francis Chadsey. Chadsey's son John ran the first ferry to bring drovers and settlers across the river and gave the town its name.

John Chads, as he called himself, strung a rope cable across the Brandywine just below Brinton's Run and pulled his ferry boat back and forth to bridge the busy road. Every horse and rider brought the ferryman four pence. Every sheep, one penny. Every hog, three half pence. Every single person on foot, three pence, and if more in the party, two pence each. Every coach, wagon or cart, one shilling and six pence. Every empty wagon or cart, nine pence.

And so it began. The traffic along Chadds Ford's stretch of U.S. Route 1 today is constant. The bridge over the Brandywine, just downstream from John Chads' bygone ferry, rumbles with 18-wheelers that nearly retrace the old drover's route. Just as Route 82, Route 322, Route 30, and the Old Strasburg Road to the north traversed the river to carry settlers west and goods east, so did Route 1.

And while the river was the reason for Chadds Ford's settlement, and the roadway the spur to its growth, the railroads helped it evolve into a quiet, but monumentally cultured town. The east-west Philadelphia and Baltimore Central Railroad, which carried wealthy

Brinton's mill

Mill stone

Philadelphians out to their summer homes, intersected the north-south Wilmington and Northern there to make Chadds Ford a natural Victorian retreat. There is no doubt that the railroad dictated Chadds Ford's destiny. As the town's character changed from rural to residential, with large Victorian mansions perched above the main road, the mills began to close. By the time the new west opened up, the Brandywine had relinquished its "Hundred Mills" nickname.

The failure of the railroad, the growth of large cities, and changes in the pattern of land ownership along the creek would lead to the closing of several mills shortly before the turn of the century. Another factor was a new invention called a roller mill which began to replace the traditional grist stone after 1880. The water wheel (which had existed at least since the first century B.C., when the writings of Marcos Vitruvius Pollio mentioned its use in Roman architecture) was growing obsolete with the turbine. Brandywine millers were practical Quakers who saw no need for the expensive overhaul of their small businesses. They couldn't compete when western milled flour dropped in price because of the new roller technology. The final blow to the larger

Mill scene

138

Brandywine mills, particularly those downstream, came during World War I, when the tons of flour previously exported to Germany were cut off. One by one, the water wheels were disconnected and the mills crumbled.

Brinton's Mill, built in 1706 where the river runs beside Route 100 and then retreats back across the plain, is one of the few that have survived. The mill's undershot water wheel turned until 1945. After it stopped, the mill sat dormant beside its stone house, and the boards gave in to age and disuse. Andrew Wyeth, who grew up with his painter father N. C. Wyeth two miles south, and was by then a famous artist in his own right, bought the mill in 1958. George Hebener, Wyeth's groundskeeper, began replacing the rotted wood and rebuilt the water wheel with a tree felled alongside Radley Run.

There is another old mill to the east along Route 1, partially restored several years ago and then boarded up, that belongs to Birmingham township. If there is a single shrine to the birth of fine art in Chadds Ford, it would have to be this pale stone building. Eighty years ago, when the Baltimore Turnpike (now four-lane Route 1) was narrow and unpaved, dusty in summer, muddy and rutted with spring rains, it was used as a painters' studio. A Philadelphian who spent his summers here at the turn of the century leased the dormant grist mill to Howard Pyle, the nephew of a former resident of the area. Chadds Ford was, in part, Pyle's inspiration in becoming the artist scholars refer to as the father of American illustration. His students used as their common studio the deserted Turner's Mill, when, near the turn of the century, Pyle volunteered to head an art academy under the auspices of the Drexel Insititute of Philadelphia.

One of Pyle's students, Newell Convers Wyeth, chose to remain in Chadds Ford and set up his own studio. Eventually he would outshine his teacher, as would his son Andrew and his grandson Jamie. N.C. Wyeth left a legacy before his untimely death at a nearby railroad crossing in 1945. His images—murals on the walls of the Metropolitan Life building in Manhattan, peaceful still lifes and landscape paintings, and illustrations that first graced the pages of adventure books, *Scribner's* and *Harper's* magazines—resound with vision. He left us with unforgettable images of Old Pew "tapping up and down the road in a frenzy and calling for his comrades" and of Robin Hood and his merry men in Sherwood Forest, rich with inspiration born of the sycamores and the magical landscapes above the Brandywine.

"Never have I appreciated nature as I have in this place," Newell Convers Wyeth said of Chadds Ford, "...this is a country full of 'restraints.' Everything lies in its subtleties, everything is so gentle and simple, so unaffected." His son Andrew, his daughters and sons-in-law, his grandson, and a multitude of area students who shared the inspiration wrought of earth, trees, and water, would all follow the passion begun in Pyle's studio. Three generations of Wyeths: N.C., Andrew, and Jamie, have loaded their palettes and carried easels alongside the Brandywine and into these meadows. Two of Andrew's sisters, Henriette Wyeth Hurd and Carolyn Wyeth, and John McCoy and Peter Hurd, who both joined the Wyeth family through marriage and the artistic talent they shared, also have passed along the valley's beauty through their art.

As is evident in Andrew Wyeth's watercolor landscapes, Chadds Ford is made of earthen tones. Particularly in autumn, when the frost bares the mottled sycamore bark, the Brandywine turns a deep loden brown and the fields rust over after harvest. Stone houses and rich riverside pasture land give the town the appearance of unshakable sturdiness.

But there is an ever-present sense of fragility about Chadds Ford. Its location, at the crossroads of U.S. Route 1 and winding Route 100, yields some of the heaviest traffic in the valley. Route 100 along the Brandywine was to have been blasted open in the 1960s, widened to four lanes like Route 1 to connect West Chester to Wilmington. The meadow near their intersection was to have been the site of a factory. The land beside the Brandywine to the south of Route 1 might have become the site of a tank farm, one of those groupings of mammoth steel hatboxes sealed to store fuel.

None of that happened in Chadds Ford. The Brandywine Conservancy, a nonprofit organization devoted to land preservation, was born in 1967 in response to the threat of industrial and commercial development along the river. An earlier attempt by residents, in 1958, to block a power company from planting a string of huge stalks carrying cable alongside the Brandywine's path, was less successful. Though the utility painted the posts the hazy green of Brandywine summers in an attempt at camouflage, they are an intrusive reminder of the changing face of the valley.

Brandywine River Museum

Boardwalk through the bog

Yet in 1967, people of Chadds Ford saved the meadow, they saved the riverside and the narrow, winding road beside its eastern bank from destruction. The Conservancy has helped to protect thousands of acres in Chester County from development through direct purchase or by persuading land owners to place deed restrictions on property. A full-time staff headquartered in Chadds Ford consults with municipalities and private developers to preserve remaining land as it is threatened.

Conserving land is not the Conservancy's only mission. The Brandywine River Museum was opened under its auspices in 1971 to preserve and provide a public exhibition place for American art. In the year of its charter, the Conservancy bought the old Hoffman's grist mill. At the time, it was a coal and lumber yard. The group converted the century-old mill, that might otherwise have been torn down, into the museum.

Outside the museum, volunteers tend wild flower gardens beside Charles Parks' sculpture "Boy With Hawk." Visitors seem to pass through the galleries of American illustration, still life and landscape paintings with a certain reverence. One wall of the museum is of glass, open to the quiet stretch of the creek, modern in its curvature of glass and poured concrete. The galleries are crisp, cool, but rich with emotion.

On the banks of the river below, a bronze cow reclines, life-sized, a duplicate of those who live in the fields upstream. That is what this museum and the Conservancy are about—a blending of man's resources with nature. New design and artistic interpretation integrated with the beauty of nature and tradition.

The freeze-thaw cycle on the river banks and rising waters threaten erosion beside the museum. A net of wire and rock holds the river bank in place and keeps the soil from slipping into the current. Beside the museum, a path leads north along the Brandywine. Boardwalks pass jewelweed turned silver after rain, turtles, and wood ducks that prefer life amongst the mire. Tiny, tender skunk cabbage shoots push through the mud just after the first spring thaw, before the butterflies arrive. Hummocks of tussock sedge, sweetflag and bullrushes reveal wetlands that allow the spring rain to seep gently into the earth, rather than cut the banks with its need to join the soil again. The path spills out onto a dry meadow, where in the early days of autumn the Chadds Ford

Ford School (and would later become Andrew Wyeth's studio), and he and his mother rented half of the house that had been Washington's headquarters in the Battle of the Brandywine. He was a lecturer and historian, a teacher at the local school in Chadds Ford. And he was a collector of the highest order during most of his eighty-four years. He first displayed his collection publicly in 1959, and when he died seven years later he left a house brimming with papers and myriad, well, things.

One of Sanderson's closest friends, Thomas R. Thompson, began an endless task of piecing through the stacks left to him. He divided the papers, the letters and books, and he cataloged the remaining items. Then Thompson hung out a shingle alongside Route 100 that announces "Christian C. Sanderson Museum," and he settled into the role of official Sanderson biographer, curator, custodian and general tour guide of the museum. With the help of some other friends, he formed a nonprofit organization to keep the collection open to visitors and to keep the memory of Chris Sanderson alive.

That white house remains a museum today. Most of its contents, cases and cases of contents, are one of a kind. There are scads of Revolutionary and Civil War items; a vial of sand from the digging of the Panama Canal; melted ice from the South Pole; a bit of bandage taken from Abraham Lincoln by a Chester County doctor who treated the president's fatal wounds. Framed on the wall of one of the downstairs rooms is a leaf taken from the wreath laid by President Wilson on the grave of Lafayette during the president's visit to Paris for the Peace Mission. There is art, including sketches and paintings given to Chris by the Wyeth family as mementos.

Discovering this tiny museum allows the pack rat in all to rejoice and share for a time the collector's lifelong fascination with memorabilia and life. His name is unfamiliar to newcomers and those passing through the village on a weekend drive; but it brings a smile to locals who remember Sanderson's hand-delivered Christmas cards and the square-dance lessons taught to local school children. Those children, grown now, recall an energetic man who played the fiddle with the same passion with which he collected bits of life and history. People leaving the house often turn to Thomas Thompson and say, "I wish I had known him."

Sanderson wrote an ode to the Brandywine. Following is an excerpt:

Tommy Thompson in his museum, Chadds Ford

The Brandywine! Stranger
    You don't know where she lies?
Well, I'll tell you, she flows through
        Southeast Pennsylvania
    Beneath the bluest of the skies;
For there the fields seem greener,
    And the trees are greener still,
And everything so quiet
    Except the ripplin' of the rills,
Until a fellow almost thinks
    That God with His Hand Divine
Must have patterned after Heaven
    When He made the old Brandywine.

147

Sanderson was the first to campaign to establish a public battlefield park surrounding the houses where Washington and Lafayette had established headquarters during the Revolutionary War. When he and his mother lived above the wooded roadside across from Pyle's studio, they nailed a "Visitors Welcome" sign on the front fence. Together they proudly guided strangers through their historic house. During their last two years there, twenty thousand names went into the Sanderson log book.

The state-administered Brandywine Battlefield Park now rolls across acres of groomed hills and includes several historic buildings and a museum. Although the actual battle took place north and west of here, the park holds the headquarters where General Washington slept prior to the fateful battle day. The old stone house that had then belonged to a Quaker farmer and miller by the name of Benjamin Ring burned to the ground in the early 1930s, but it has since been reconstructed to a nearly exact reproduction. At the Gideon Gilpin house across a rise to the east, the nineteen-year-old Marquis de Lafayette was quartered. He saw here at Chadds Ford his first military action in America.

Thousands of soldiers re-enact the battle in the fields above the Brandywine each year, beginning with an encampment and a skirmish in the park. It is not authentic—since the battle was not fought on park lands—but for show. On a September afternoon, a young squirrel, accustomed to the usual serenity of the park, sees his first military action. He darts frantically amid the musket fire and cannon, so disoriented that he scampers atop a huddle of felled soldiers as if to mimic the women and young boys who hurriedly bring water to the men and help the wounded from the field.

The actual battlegrounds are peaceful today, except for the occasional grind of the bulldozer and rhythmic hammer where new roads called "Lafayette Blvd." or "Revolutionary Dr." have sprouted houses. A stone house of worship built long and low in 1763 by those early Quaker families stands on the hill above the Brandywine. Fallen revolutionary soldiers are buried in the wooded graveyard beside Birmingham Friends Meeting, in the shadow of a high granite shaft that honors Lafayette, who was wounded not far away. Soldiers once lay dying here as the smoke and rumbling fire of artillery settled heavy in the valley below, at the Battle of the Brandywine. The skirmish took the creek's name because the water would prove to be the betrayer of battle.

The redcoats were coming in 1777. Three weeks after William Bradley sent his dispatch that the British had anchored a hundred ships at the Patapsco River, they were on their way to battle. British General William Howe chose a circuitous route, expecting to find fewer civilian enemies amongst the people of Maryland's Cecil County and the pacifist Quaker lands of lower Pennsylvania. The soldiers left the waters of the Chesapeake Bay and landed at the Head of Elk to begin their march toward Philadelphia. First, they would have to ford the Brandywine. Washington's troops were there, readying their defense.

In addition to staving off an attack on the city, General Washington also intended to protect the iron deposits, the furnaces, farms, and mills along the river. The opposing armies were stationed on opposite sides of the Brandywine as the Americans fought to hold the fords. Particularly Chadds Ford, with its crossing on the main road to Philadelphia that is now U.S. Route 1. Local efforts to reinforce the Continental Army were tremendous. Any man between the ages of eighteen and fifty-three was called to fight. every male member of the Forks of the Brandywine Church on the upper West Branch joined the rebellion. Whole towns joined in the fight for autonomy. And as the forces marched off, the women took over the fields, raised their children alone in anticipation of the battle's end, and many became widows.

Some eleven thousand American soldiers under Washington tried to keep General Howe's eighteen thousand men from crossing the Brandywine at Chadds Ford. Once they crossed the river, the Tories could move rapidly toward Philadelphia. By placing detachments of troops at what he thought were the southern and northernmost crossings of the Brandywine, Washington guessed he would divert the British troops to Chadds Ford, where his men were stationed and ready. Many were initiated to battle that September morning in 1777, when a heavy fog covered the hill to the east of the creek.

But while one of Howe's contingents marched from Kennett Square toward well-protected Chadds Ford, the majority crossed north of the rebels' northernmost guard at Wistar's Ford. They crossed instead at Trimble's Ford near Northbrook on the West Branch, followed by

Jefferis Ford on the East Branch, and then marched due south into the flank of the American forces. The British were able to gain a strategic position in Birmingham by mid-afternoon.

The attack was a complete surprise.

Washington ordered his army to take the high ground at Birmingham Meeting as a last defense, and nightfall brought the battle to an end. As the Americans quickly retreated to Chester, Howe's exhausted troops celebrated their complete victory by emptying the tavern's liquor supply. They camped on the battlefield, moved into the Quaker farmyards and pillaged grain stores. And as they marched on toward Philadelphia, they left dead farm animals and ransacked homes in their wake. Despite his efforts to recover food and supplies, Washington was unable to recuperate the losses at Chadds Ford. As he retreated to Chester, farmers and innkeepers began to inventory their cows, flour and grain, and to count their losses.

Worse yet, the British marched into Philadelphia unopposed on September 26. The loss ultimately led to the occupation of both Wilmington and Philadelphia during the winter of 1777, while the Continental Army battled the elements in Valley Forge. The Brandywine was, of course, no Waterloo. As with the battles of Long Island and White Plains, the loss of this major battle was not conclusive; the war continued and the Revolution was won.

Beyond the heavy concrete bridge that carries Route 1 traffic across the Brandywine at Chadds Ford, the river grows fuller with the input of Ring Run, Harvey Run and Wilson Run. It widens into slow backwaters, switches east, grows wide with a turn toward flat land, and then the river passes beneath a gray concrete viaduct. The WPA bridge, grown beautiful with age, spans first a meadow and then the river. It has been known locally, since the day when two wooden bridges crossed here in tandem, as the Twin Bridges.

The Brandywine twists through a wooded glen, below meadows of yarrow and Queen Anne's lace, wild pinks, sumac and the New England asters that bloom in late summer with the goldenrod. Those are the subjects of one of George A. Weymouth's best-known paintings. He travels the world to paint portraits, yet here he sketches the skeletal snags of trees that have died upright in the wetlands and the beautiful weeds and wildflowers that are given all-out freedom across the fields here at Big Bend, his home. "Frolic," as he is known by friends, sits at

Window, Brandywine Battlefield State Park

the head of the board of trustees of the Brandywine Conservancy.

He lives in a sturdy, elegant, stone house on the site of a one-time Indian trading post. Big Bend was a village called "Queonemysing" when the Indians held this land. A chief named Sectarius led his people of the Unami group of the Lenni-Lenape here, and their totem, a turtle, has become Weymouth's totem, too. The turtle marks the gates to his mile-long driveway, and, in brass, the leather harnesses hung from his tack room walls. Queonemysing was the most important documented village of the Indians, a fishing village until mill dams prevented shad from coming upstream. Antique carriages line the courtyard of Weymouth's bank barn, where he stables a team of bay Standardbreds, bred by Lancaster County Amishmen. He drives four-in-hand, fording the lower waters of the Brandywine beside his house to pass along the Indian trails to the south. Despite his efforts and successes at land

Backwaters, Chadds Ford

Swamp with lily pads

preservation, Weymouth, too, feels the pangs of development as it swallows his neighbors' fields. A favorite carriage trail has been cleared and paved and lined with new houses. A street sign that marks its meeting with the once secluded stretch of Bullock Road reads, ironically, "Carriage Path Drive."

From Big Bend, the Indians' "Rattlesnake Trail" led across the creek to Point Lookout. It trailed south to the first Swedish settlement on the Christina River in Wilmington, then grew over with vines and fallen trees when the Delaware tribe sold to William Penn the land between Chester Creek and Christina Creek in December 1683. Once the headquarters of the Vicmead Hunt Club, the estate at Point Lookout is now home to Jamie Wyeth and his wife, Phyllis.

At the bend, the Brandywine dips just below the Delaware border,

Twin bridges

Frolic's four-in-hand

and then as if to say, "One more look at Pennsylvania," it pushes its current briefly north and then declines steadily toward the tidewater that waits some fifteen miles south. The border between the states is a perfect arc, the only round border in the nation. It was laid out from a point when Penn's colony was to have been equidistant from New Castle, Delaware. A pair of surveyors named Isaac Taylor and Thomas Person marked and measured the curved line at the turn of the eighteenth century. They cut the bark from the border trees to record their boundary. In time the cuts disappeared, their painstaking work dissolved, until the boundary was surveyed again in 1892 and marked with more lasting stones.

From here to Smith Bridge, named for Isaac Smith who ran a succession of mills (flour and grist, saw and cider press) powered by the race, the Brandywine is a pretty waif hidden amongst trees. Some of the locusts and oaks are standing, others fallen, decaying to earth. A pathway cuts through brush and over high outcroppings of rocks and then the land opens at the bridge; a clearing, evenly mown and parklike in comparison to the woods and fields to the north. And the houses, unlike the nearly camouflaged orange and brown stone houses of the Quaker farmers, are massive estates the color of black gun-powder, perched securely on hilltops.

Water tower, Granogue

160

Silo, Granogue

Pont purchased a one-time Penn grant parcel on which a Quaker family had created one of America's first arboretums. Today the endowment of the former chairman of the Du Pont Company and General Motors provides for much of his thousand-acre estate's annual budget. The remainder comes from memberships and admission charged the million visitors who walk through the gardens and sprawling greenhouses each year.

Henry Francis du Pont collected furniture. Roughly 83,000 decorative American objects. Winterthur Museum, the nine-story French-style mansion he built to hold his collection, is his legacy. Hidden in a valley of trees beside Route 52, it is neatly wrapped in a two-hundred-acre display garden. On the southern side of the Winterthur woods, above a pond that fills with hundreds of Canada Geese at the turning of the seasons, there is a small wooden sign. From the hilltop, before the white gazebo on the rise to the east of the hills and farms that trail off beyond, the sign reads:

Keep this view open forever.
    H.F. du Pont 1964

Not a request, rather a command. The growth and development of this valley, spurred on largely by the industry the du Pont family forged, had become a threat. Even to the legacy of a man who tissued his estate in acreage, boxed it in boundary lines and decorated it with beautiful plants. And so this man who inspired the Winterthur Museum, the authoritative resource for studying American furnishings and decorative art, left his mark not only on the interiors, but on land across the valley, beside the Brandywine.

While a large portion of Winterthur was a working farm where du Pont's men grew vegetables and raised animals, he searched for a separate place to keep his dairy cows. He chose land to the east, well out of noseshot of his genteel estate. Two hundred head of cattle grazed in an upper pasture there while his workers harvested wheat and corn on the lower ground. This land has since become Delaware's Brandywine Creek State Park, where a few hundred thousand people drive through the gate each year to roam its eight hundred acres.

The parkland along the Brandywine is wooded, the high land coated in pale grass. Clashing air masses heave billowing cumulus clouds above the hills, and dark granite walls, four feet high, define the fields. The Baltimore gneiss and Wissahickon schist of Chester County to the north has given way here to a range of harder igneous rock, called gabbro—a rock that has been called the granite of Brandywine commerce for its use in constructing the mills downstream. In the park, the gabbro was sheered straight and topped with heavy uncut cap stones which have held the walls in place for a century.

In 1893, after crews had finished work on Winterthur, Henry Francis du Pont paid Italian stone masons a dollar a day to build these fences. In fact, rumor had it that he spent more money putting up the walls than on the purchase of this land itself. It wasn't unusual for the du Ponts to employ master builders for such projects—to keep them employed between larger projects at their mills or larger estates. Examples of their craftsmanship are scattered along the river's course south.

Henry Francis du Pont built farm buildings along the southern edge of his eastern farm between 1900 and 1940, some with American chestnuts killed by blight. The chestnut, prized for its sweet fruits, its tannin, and hardwood that vied with oak as America's favorite, proved susceptible to a deadly blight imported in the early 1900s on Chinese chestnut trees planted in New York. Within decades the disease spread through American cities and forests, strangling an estimated nine million acres of trees.

The tenant farmer who worked the sloping fields above the wooded banks of the Brandywine in 1910 was paid $30 a month, along with use of the house, firewood, and four quarts of milk a day. The livestock emphasis changed from cattle to pigs in the late fifties, and the farm changed hands within the du Pont family until 1960 when Ellen du Pont Wheelright took control of the 435 acres there.

Mrs. Wheelright offered the land to the public in 1964, and it became the first state park built with matching use of federal land and water conservation funds. A nature center was built, the roads paved, and the habitats—tulip tree woods with 175-year-old giants, a fresh-water marsh, and a 90-acre stand of white oak—were made accessible with trails. Tulip Tree Woods, its 24 acres undisturbed for two centuries, has been set aside as a nature preserve by the Delaware Division of Parks and Recreation. The status provides legal protection to areas that have a special natural history or are home to rare plants

Stone wall, Brandywine Creek State Park

and animals.

The park's twelve miles of trails from Thompson Bridge to Rockland on the east side of the river are the legacy of another land holder, William Poole Bancroft. Park administrators worked a purchase donation from the Woodlawn Trust to add another 350 acres to the park in 1983. The trust was incorporated after Bancroft's profitable textile mill downstream enabled him before his death in 1928 to "gather up the rough land along the Brandywine above Rockland and hold it for the future of Wilmington." Some of the land he left to the discretion of the trustees was to remain public parkland. And as industry in his day was posing a threat to residential building, his wish was also to provide land for homes in the valley. Development of some portions of the enormous trust enabled the Woodlawn Trustees to purchase new land above Wilmington and keep some of the roads, edged with crumbling farm houses, clear water, and dense forests, free from the sort of commercial growth seen to the east along Route 202.

Along the eastern half of the park, where a footpath follows the

Field with hay

Maples, Brandywine Creek State Park

Page 167: Rockland Dam

river south from Thompson Bridge, the land was first inhabited by the Lenni-Lenape Indians. When English settlers pushed inland from Wilmington in the late-seventeenth century, they found the Brandywine's tributaries made excellent races for milling. Beaver Run, to the north, once powered a paper mill, a clover mill, a mill for Turkish carpets, and a woolen mill. The miller of wool, Zachariah Crease, nearly washed away with a flood in August 1843 because he so cherished the place of his livelihood. He refused to evacuate until the water had invaded the second floor. Trout Run, a tributary of Beaver Run, was loud with the mechanics of a tool factory in those early days of industry.

Another miller, William Wilson, gave his name to Wilson Run in the eighteenth century. Later, ice would be cut from the ponds beside his stream, packed in sawdust and shipped south to Savannah and other southern cities where it could remain frozen in storage for as long as four months. Today Wilson Run is a cool stream in spring for trout fishermen, while the Brandywine anglers cast for crappies, bluegill, and rock bass.

The sound of wide, spilling water grows louder until the trail opens to a clearing beside the large dam at Rockland. Before the railroad, six-mule teams pulled wagons full of raw materials and finished products from a cotton mill on the west bank across this place that was once called Kirk's Ford for a family of millers who worked here before the Revolution. William Young started his papermill at Rockland shortly before 1800. There he succeeded in making paper from mulberry wood, for which he was awarded a gold medal by the Philadelphia Booksellers. Today the Rockland Road crosses below the dam and winds above a colony of condominiums, some converted from the old mills and miller's houses, to follow the high ground above the east bank.

Turn-of-the-century Brandywine observer Wilmer MacElree, when he reached this spot in his journey down the river, wrote, "Yes, this is Rockland, and in front of you is Rockland Dam. You have now advanced as far as you can go. A little distance below the land belongs to the du Ponts."

MacElree was correct. The land below has long been off limits to the public, with the exception of the Wilmington Trails Club, formed in 1938 for people the likes of founding member Clayton Hoff who felt that the best way to see the Brandywine was to get out and hike it. Members continue to set out along these banks, after the fashion of MacElree and Frank R. Zebley, the former Speaker of the House of Delaware's General Assembly who in 1941 published a book he researched between legislative sessions. Zebley's book is entitled *Along the Brandywine: A chronicle compiled from observations and inquiries made during the leisure of five summers.*

Since MacElree's observation at the turn of the century, and Zebley's chronicles forty years later, the land beside the Brandywine has changed little. Massive houses have passed on to a second or perhaps a third generation within the du Pont family. In the small gorge beyond the Rockland Dam the water crouches, then hides from public view as it passes behind the well-guarded estate of Pierre (Pete) du Pont, the former governor of Delaware. Beyond a thick cover of woods, it flows toward Louviers, another French-style du Pont estate that has been in the family since 1811.

When the sprawling yellow house was built, a small boat attached to wire ferried workers and residents across the river to the west bank. While on a return visit to the land of his first battle, an elderly Marquis de Lafayette made the journey here. When his host led him to the steep hill above the eastern bank, his breath grew weak and he requested a less strenuous path. From that day, the rise was known as "Lafayette's Path." Later a pair of planks floating atop barrels, hinged in the middle, was laid across the river here. Disconnected with heavy rains to swing to the banks and be spared the damage of late-winter freshets. A wooden bridge followed, and finally the Iron Bridge that crosses now.

The bridge is now closed with the solitude of the east bank. An overgrown mill race and a crumpled foundation are all that are left of the Du Pont-Bauduy woolen mill that once stood nearby. Coopers made powder kegs of wood on this slope. A powder plant built on this bank to keep up with demand during the Spanish-American War is gone, as is another nearby woolen mill that furnished cloth to the government during the War of 1812. And the simple concrete buildings that grew here for experimental purposes during World War I have also fallen. In fact, a row of stone houses called Chicken Alley is all that remains of a village that grew up from an old stone woolen mill.

After Louviers come the rock fields; hikers here must scale a half mile of granite boulders that burst from the spongy soil. The private trails along the water here are silent, and yet across the river, beside Holly Island, runs a millrace that once powered a frightfully busy powder yard. Because the Brandywine drops 120 feet in its final four miles, there was terrific potential for industry from here to tidewater in the eighteenth and nineteenth centuries. Nearly every type of mill product was made along the river at one time or another.

Flour and gunpowder first became great American industries here. Paper in rolls was first manufactured here, then textiles, then the synthetic organic materials that remain the foremost products of the Du Pont Company. Cellophane, paints, plastics and dyes, explosives, insecticides, medical equipment, nylon, Dacron and Teflon. All are the products descended from the first powder mills founded beside the Brandywine. Du Pont today is the world's largest chemical manufacturer, with more than a hundred plants in the U.S. and corporate and industrial branches throughout the world. The du Pont family itself has produced a lineage of statesmen, of U.S. senators, a state governor and presidential hopeful, military officers, and, of course, leaders of business and industry.

Eleuthere Irenee du Pont (1771-1834), a student of the famous French chemist Antoine Lavoisier, left France because of the political unrest in which he and his father, Pierre Samuel du Pont de Nemours, had taken part. His father was a statesman who after studying medicine in France had turned to economic affairs, spurred on by the conflicts that followed the French Revolution. While in his native country Pierre had an active correspondence with Benjamin Franklin and Thomas Jefferson, and he knew that opportunity awaited in America. He would later return to France, but E. I. du Pont would never leave Wilmington.

Fledgling America was well on its way. But he observed there was a void to be filled. In 1802, E. I. du Pont took up sixty-five acres along the west bank of the Brandywine to build Eleutherian Mills, a stately house and a gunpowder yard. Within two years E. I. du Pont de Nemours & Company—sandwiched between the grist, paper and textile mills to the north and an active flour-shipping trade to the south—was on its way to becoming the nation's largest manufacturer of gunpowder. To meet an increased demand for black powder during the War of 1812, E. I. du Pont, known better as Irenee, purchased a neighboring tract of land to the south known as Hagley. There he built a second powder

Hagley mills

quarry now face the water. Across from them is the last remaining mill in production on the lower Brandywine.

The Wilmington Finishing Company, where workers run fabric through water brought up from the river, is descended from a textile mill begun more than 170 years ago. Its many faces of brick and steel, stucco and concrete, form an unbroken wall along the river. A melange of building materials signifying additions to a business that began with a simple mill built by a Quaker immigrant.

Leaving behind his large family and any semblance of stability, John Bancroft set sail for America in 1821 with a group of fellow Quakers from Lancashire and Cheshire. His chairmaking business was a success, and his letters home encouraged the rest of his family to join him. The Bancrofts packed what they could onto a ship and set sail for Wilmington, where John Bancroft's father took up a partnership in a small flannel mill near the mouth of the Brandywine. When John's brother Joseph arrived in the summer of 1824, having finished an apprenticeship in England, they were all together again—father, mother, and thirteen children under a single roof.

Though the latest to arrive, Joseph would prove to be the most industrious. With borrowed capital from a wealthy backer, he bought fifty acres of land and one-half of the water rights on a stretch of the Brandywine just below Rockford. He went to work repairing the dam, enlarging the race, and readying a small mill to loom cloth. He built the miller's houses that are now elegant row homes above the river, and the company stores. Ten years into production, a flood wiped out the mills. Waters rose twenty-two feet, taking looms and warps, carding engines and drying equipment. Floods caused by melting snows and huge slabs of jammed ice were a recurring threat to all of the millers along the river. Historical accounts and letters often refer to flood damage and the washout of bridges.

Joseph Bancroft rebuilt his mills and took his sons William and Samuel into a partnership that would later be known as Joseph Bancroft & Sons, Co. Their determination, reflected in a willingness to put in seventy hours of labor at the shops a week, pushed the business through hard times. They plowed through the1857 financial panic—set off by the closing of the Ohio Life and Trust Companies—that took a devastating toll on merchants and millers along the eastern seaboard. After their father died in 1874 of pneumonia, Samuel and William

Page 178: Bancroft mill

Bancroft ably ran Bancroft Mills.

Both men were philanthropists, yet the brothers led disparate lives. Samuel mingled with artists and the literary set, who inspired the mill's book cloth dyeing business. His first order was, in fact, produced for the binding of Bayard Taylor's *Prince Dekalion.* His legacy is the collection of the pre-Raphaelite paintings that hangs in the Delaware Art Museum upriver from the mill.

William, on the other hand, lived simply, dressed plainly, and unlike his brother, was a strict Quaker. His interests lay not in worldliness but in the gradual accumulation of land. He was instrumental in forming the Wilmington Board of Park Commissioners, following William Marriot Canby to serve as president from 1904 to 1923. He gave generously to private schools and colleges, the Delaware Hospital and the Wilmington Library. He gave because he liked people. And because he had a love for the land, he endowed a part of his farm to the city of Wilmington in 1889 with the wish of seeing a park established there. That land became Rockford Park. He watched Wilmington grow, and in the twenty years prior to the turn of the century, William Bancroft bought land that he considered valuable for parkland and held it until the mayor and city council could be persuaded to acquire it. He often accepted payment for less than the cost of the original purchase, and it is estimated that he gave more than 220 acres outright to the city for parks. When he was sixty-six, Bancroft organized the Woodlawn Trust, the company that would carry out his ambitious plans beyond his lifetime.

The finishing mills continued after William Bancroft's death in 1928, and after recovering from the shortages of dyes, fuel, cloth, and manpower resulting from World War I, the stock market crash of 1929 sent the mills into a financial tailspin from which they didn't recover for a full decade. During World War II, the mill turned over its famous process of bleaching, mercerizing, shrinking, printing, dyeing and finishing cotton and rayon goods to the government to outfit the armed forces. According to a 1946 article in the Wilmington *Sunday Morning Star*, the wartime outfitting required more than a hundred different fabrics. The output ranged from burlap for protective sandbags, to bookcloths for binding textbooks and manuals, and duck carrying-bags, to dinner napkins and tablecloths. In all, Bancroft processed over 425 million yards of fabrics for war purposes, devoting nearly three-fourths of its production to the task. In the years since the war, the plant has changed hands twice, production has slowed, and large parts of the building have been sold for uses other than manufacturing.

A clever writer for the *Saturday Evening Post* once dubbed Wilmington "America's first 'boom' town." The double entendre fits, whether in view of gunpowder or the many other goods produced here. Unlike so many milling and factory towns, Wilmington fared well aesthetically during the industrial revolution. The mills left no indelible scar on the landscape. The brick and stone mills weren't replaced by gargantuan hulks of black steel. The trees were not cleared in mass from the riverside, and those banks that were cleared have returned to leafy forest again. There is such mystique and sentiment about the river above Wilmington that development there is minimal. Most local developers today would sooner pay to renovate an old mill than tear down and begin again. They would sooner battle the challenge of old age, transforming a mill like the old Bancroft place with its inevitable leaks and cracks, its limited access and obscure location, than see it fall to rubble.

Charles Parks lives and works in Building 44 of the old Bancroft works. He, too, is an artist who takes inspiration from the water, working clay into the busts and statues, the people of this place and ecclesiastical sculptures. The sculptures return from the foundry in gleaming yellow bronze to take on a sturdy, dark patina before they leave the studio.

Just below the site of Rockford Mills, Joshua and Thomas Gilpin built a paper mill in 1787, where they pressed paper by hand, one sheet at a time. Thirty years later, Thomas invented a machine to make continuous roll paper, which he supplied to the *American Daily Advertiser* in Philadelphia and other journals. He secured a patent, and envious competitors began bribing workmen for his secrets, which they would adapt just enough to avoid prosecution.

Meanwhile, Joshua Gilpin was the first paper maker in America to use a new chemical to bleach rags, a process he learned while visiting Europe. Beginning in 1804, he began sorting the cotton and linen, washing, bleaching, and macerating it to press fine paper. It took one and a half pounds of rags to make a pound of the paper that carried the Gilpin watermark. The mark which showed through the paper read "Brandywine," and it signified quality. His plant was destroyed by fire

Bridge over the Brandywine

182

Beneath Washington Street Bridge

Spil

Wilmington's Brandywine Park begins where these millers lived. The land, beginning its descent along what here become the north and south banks as the river turns eastward, is said to be compiled from some forty separate deeds. A meeting was held in 1868 to discuss a public park along the Brandywine and the city council moved to purchase the land, but an injunction obtained by taxpayers who objected to the expense halted the project. More than ten years passed before the idea of a riverside park was revived, a board of park commissioners appointed, and the land preserved.

Below the old Baltimore and Ohio Railroad Bridge, Rattlesnake Run joins the flow. At the end of North Park Drive, a large building of modern condominiums marks the end of the park. A net of steel cable and concrete called the swinging bridge, stretched so that people might cross the river, overlooks a supply dam and the beginning of a race that will line the west bank for a mile or so. A pair of races once ran along either side of the dam, built first to supply power for mills at Brandywine Village. While the north race has been filled, the south now performs the initial cleaning for the city's water supply. Spillovers control the level of the race, forming dam-like waterfalls. A sycamore tree grips the side of one, its upper branches as white as bleached bone, its roots black as the saturated rocks they grasp. Those roots, too, become the trace for the falls where the music that the water makes drowns out the fleeting traffic on the interstate highway bridge that cuts high above the gorge.

North Park Drive scoots beside the east bank of the Brandywine, beside Tatnall's Woods, now the Brandywine Zoo, where a black bear, like the ones that used to roam the wooded hills above the river, rolls in his cage. The road passes beneath great bridges that span the ravine carved out by the river. The Washington Street bridge, which would look fitting should it span the Seine, crosses high above the First Dam which was built to supply water for the mills below.

Another pair of races once led from the lower dam to join the two from the Third Dam upstream. A village of restored houses covers the higher ground to the east, this old milling town beside the east bank known as Brandywine Village. A settlement sewn from the spirit of a woman named Elizabeth Shipley.

As a Quaker minister, traveling through Pennsylvania to various Friends' meetings to witness her faith in the 1730s, Shipley had a powerful vision. She dreamed she was traveling through the wilds and came upon the vista of two rivers, one shallow, rocky and swift, the other deep and slow-moving—the two joined together on a flat plain. On a visit to Friends' meetings south of her Pennsylvania home, Elizabeth Shipley saw the place of her dream. There, in counties ceded to Penn in a special grant by James, Duke of York, so that Penn could control the approach to Pennsylvania by sea, the roads were crude, little more than Indian trails. She came to a ford on the Brandywine beside a barley mill. There she crossed the turbulent stream on horseback and climbed a hill, where looking west she could see calmer and deeper water, the low coastal plain of the Christina River.

She returned to tell her husband of the land, still so wild, with only a few farmhouses and a small, stone Swedish Lutheran Church. When William Shipley heard his wife's news he was skeptical, yet curious. He was dissatisfied with farming, and he had longed to become a merchant since first sailing into Philadelphia's busy port. He thought the area Elizabeth described might become a shipping center for farm produce.

Shipley went to see the place between the rivers in 1735 and met a man by the name of Thomas Willing. The entrepreneur was laying out plots on his property along the Christina for a town to be called Willingtown. William Shipley bought several lots, built a large home, and brought with him several of his neighbors from the Springfield and Ridley areas near Philadelphia. Within two years, Willingtown was a village of thirty homes. Shipley and his townsmen had taken their choice parcels along the Brandywine, where they could ship wheat and grains grown from the northern fields to Philadelphia, or to the West Indies and Europe.

Soon the members of this newly formed village petitioned King George II for a charter whereby their town could become self-governing and hold markets. The King granted their request, but with one stipulation. The town was to be renamed Wilmington, in honor of his friend George Spencer-Compton, Earl of Wilmington, England.

Oliver Canby built the first gristmill on the lower Brandywine, just below the King's Road that led from Philadelphia to Baltimore, in 1742. The busy turnpike was an opportune place to buy grain or to sell meal and flour. He ground the farmland grain to flour so fine and whole that it was shipped to Boston, New York, and Charleston for fine pastries

Pages 188, 189: Wilmington skyline

and other delectables. Before long, ships loaded with Canby's flour were setting sail from the Delaware Bay for Martinique, LaHavre, Antwerp, Calcutta, Java, Lisbon, and Belfast, and returning to Wilmington with cargos of fine chocolate, coffee, and wines. Through the eighteenth and nineteenth centuries, several other mills were built along the banks of the lower Brandywine. Widows walks atop grand houses attest to its history as a port. The mills and warehouses here were accessible to the greatest grain regions in the country. Ships carrying up to two thousand bushels of wheat could moor at the mills, others in the Christina.

The farmers of the upper Brandywine hauled their grain to the mills for processing, or to the mouth of the river to be shipped out. They developed a heavy wagon, a Conestoga, named for a region belonging to the Minquas tribe that first laid the route east of the Brandywine along Route 202 between Wilmington and West Chester. The six-horse wagon, with its wooden frame and cloth cover, could haul vast amounts of grain to market, and twenty to thirty of the sturdy rigs would sometimes flank the mills. The same wagon, invented strictly to get grain to the Brandywine, later hauled goods and families west across the Alleghenies as America grew. The "prairie schooner" eventually sailed on to the Santa Fe, California, and Oregon trails. Together with the log cabin, which was also born in the Brandywine Valley, the covered wagon became a symbol of American settlement and westward expansion.

When Wilmington's millers shipped processed flour to the West Indies, the boats returned with cargos of rum and molasses. Soon they developed cooperative standards for their products and created the most successful early example of line production in America. Brandywine millers, reviving trade after the Revolution, organized joint inspection of the products of all their mills to standardize the quality and weight of their flour. The flour was shipped under the trade name "Brandywine Mills," which, like the Gilpin watermark, became a mark of distinction and commanded the highest price. By the end of the eighteenth century, the American price of wheat and flour was determined on the Brandywine, in the same way that the price of steel was set in Pittsburgh for decades.

Today, on the east side of the Brandywine below the Market Street bridge, the foundations of an old mill of brick and stone have been topped with newly constructed condominiums. The street is Superfine Lane, where the finest flour available was once ground. From here to river's end, the water is twenty feet deep through a narrow channel. Water spills in from the Delaware Bay to form a five-foot tide, and blue crabs stalk the bottom of the Brandywine.

The North Park Drive that followed through the shaded Brandywine Park ends abruptly. Across the water there is a city, a small city with an impressive skyline. Blue glass and concrete and steel mount up like oblong quartz crystals; Wilmington is geometry against the sky. At the base of that cityscape, people sit at dinner tables in a renovated wing of the old waterworks building. Beneath them, a thick white spray of water tumbles to the slowing river. The waterworks, which still provides Wilmington with Brandywine drinking water, is a remnant of the age of grand industrial architecture. The pumping station and filtration plant were built upon the foundations of old mills, just as the city itself grew from the groundwork laid by former millers. The plant buildings were designed in the Roman style of the Chicago World's Fair during the first decade of the twentieth century. Three Palladian windows look out across the creek on one side, three face the road with the letters PVMPING STATION chiseled into the flat local granite above the door. Utilitarian in function, grandiose in form.

The city's public works department is two centuries old. The first resolution introduced in borough council in 1796 provided for a committee "to inquire of the inhabitants of the borough who owned pumps which stood in the street, whether they would be willing to give them to the corporation who would take care to have them kept in order." And so the Wilmington Spring Water Company was incorporated in 1804. The borough bought it six years later for $10,000, forming one of the earliest municipal water departments in the country, the Wilmington Water Department. With the purchase of water rights and a mill property on the Brandywine, the first pump raised water to a reservoir at Rodney Square—the highest point in the city—in 1827. The system was similar to that installed for the Philadelphia Water Works at Fairmount Park Station with the pump itself operated by water power, the current falling over forty buckets on an overshot wheel.

While the lower Brandywine was once most useful as a power generator for individual mills, it is now primarily a supplier of public water. The largest water supplier of the Christina River Basin, which is formed together with the White Clay and Red Clay Creeks to the northwest and the Christina River, the Brandywine is the most valuable of the creeks and rivers in the basin. While seventy percent of its drainage area is in Chester County, seventy percent of the river's use as a water supply is designated for New Castle County.

The river supplies half of New Castle County's water, and when needed the New Castle Water Resources Authority turns over additional water to adjacent communities with less abundant sources. The City of Wilmington relies on the Brandywine for ninety-six percent of its drinking water. Wilmington's water is diverted by a low dam downstream from the Augustine Cutoff bridge. When it reaches the Brandywine Pumping Station at Sixteenth and Market Streets, it has flowed by gravity for nearly a mile through South Brandywine Park, along the masonry race first built by the millers. The station pumps the raw water up from the race to the Brandywine Filtration Plant, and finished water through a network of water mains underground to reservoirs and towers.

A backup water supply is seldom needed. Yet heavy rains sometimes kick up chocolate brown turbidity too thick with silt. Then the water resources authority turns to a line run from the Edgar M. Hoopes Reservoir, a two-billion-gallon preserve to the west. Filled by runoff from its watershed and water that is pumped from the Brandywine for storage, the reservoir beside Red Clay Creek can supply up to twelve million gallons a day.

Wilmington's water supply system was designed and built for 140,000 residents. Now, with urban sprawl and a general tendency for business to overpower residential building in Wilmington, there are only about 70,000 city inhabitants. Two filter plants—one beside Market Street, another two miles to the west along Concord Pike—clean the water before it travels through 334 miles of transmission and distribution piping to industries and businesses, houses, and fire hydrants.

Unlike Chester County, there is no flood control along the Brandywine in Delaware. There is no need, as the drop increases and the banks break wider. A gauge at the state line measures stream flow, which is dependent upon the actions of the Chester County Water Resources Authority upstream. Wilmington's Department of Public

Works was once most concerned about the dropping flow in seasons of lean rain. With the creation of the Marsh Creek and the Hoopes reservoirs, those fears have eased. Yet, as high density development continues in Pennsylvania, groundwater depletion and reduced stream flow threaten the entire watershed.

And, with that development, the water *quality* is threatened by increased discharges. No longer because of factories; regulations concerning industrial effluent have nearly removed that threat from the entire length of the river. The Delaware River Basin Commission oversees all effluent, and there are no permits requested from the Commission or the State Geological Survey to discharge anything into the creek below the Delaware state line. New development in Chester County, rather—the sewage treatment plant and eroding soil—are threatening water quality along the length of the Brandywine.

Wilmington's own waste disposal is handled by an old system of combining sewage with effluent and runoff flowing through a single pipe that runs to the Wilmington Treatment Plant at Cherry Island. After treatment, waste water is discharged into the Delaware River beyond the Brandywine.

Machine-tool builders and car repair shops line the water's edge where the Brandywine Creek Bridge weaves its green iron lattice across at 14th Street. The world from the bridge is gray. A power plant across the marshland, gray buildings, a crane that lifts crumpled metal atop the gray mountains of salvaged scrap. In the distance, the slate steeple of the Cathedral Church of St. John pierces the sky above Brandywine Village. There is no color except for the playground beside the bridge, where children dressed in vibrant pink, blue and yellow climb up the metal bars and run between the worn patches of grass and the dirt trampled hard as stone. Beside the water, patchy sycamores lean toward their reflections.

While cars shoot across the Church Street Bridge, the Interstate 495 bridge supports a silhouette of trucks high above a distant marsh. An Amtrak train crosses its trestle southward along the waning creek. It follows the path of the Pennsylvania Railroad Drawbridge, stretched from bank to bank a century and a half ago, when steamers were new and the rails brought promise of future enterprise to this land.

The draw bridge, the final crossing-place before the river ends, has through the years seen prosperity and hardship. The waters once rose up to carry the iron trestle away toward the sea in 1869. And one foggy morning in the early 1880s, the lift operator raised the rebuilt bridge to allow a barge to pass below, oblivious to an approaching peach train. The brakeman tried, but couldn't stop his train until the locomotive was dangling over the edge—it teetered for a second or two—and then the heavy engine plunged like a walrus from an ice floe into the dark water. No one was injured, and the engineer and fireman, no doubt shaken, jumped to safety on the deck of the barge below.

The mouth of the Brandywine once meandered pellmell through flatlands when Wilmington first grew from the land between the Delaware and Christina rivers. It is now constricted to a utilitarian wasteland beyond the waterworks. There is no parkland or grass, there are no more perky beeches, no spot to pull the car beside a shoal and watch the water flow. The creek passes a narrow line of scruffy shrubs and thin trees now, where Dutch coopers made kegs in the mid-1600s, and past the place where a lost creek called Black Cats Kill once took cover beneath deep banks and entered the waters.

It is certain that this is where the Brandywine was named, but questionable as to why the water was so poetically christened. There are accounts that a Dutch ship carrying kegs of golden wine sank at the mouth of the creek, and that its confluence with the water conferred the name. Similar to that tale is the story that it was a keg-laden wagon, not a boat, that slid down a bank and emptied its cargo into the waters.

But most historians hold another theory, that the Brandywine was named not for a golden libation, but for a Dutch settler. The earliest settlers of the lower counties traditionally named their rivers after a person who lived along the banks near the mouth of the waterway. Historians claim the Brandywine is shown by old records to have been called by Dutch settlers "Fishkill," until a grant to a Dutchman named Andren Brainwinde who is said to have owned two hundred acres on the south side of the creek in 1670. "Brainwinde's Kill" (or creek) was evidently corrupted through time to the anglicized Brandywine.

Revolution and persecution abroad, and yellow fever in the quickly developing city of Philadelphia, first brought the Swedes and Finns here in 1638. Settlement began on a patch of land beside the close of the Brandywine, just up the Christina as it flows into the three-mile-wide estuary of the Delaware River. When the Swedes, and later the Dutch, sailed into the Brandywine to unload their ships, the joint estuary of the Brandywine and the Christina off the well-traveled Delaware made an ideal trading port and encouraged emigration. The Christina's water winds wide and deep for seven miles and ends having had little drop. Not ideal for powering industry, but well navigable, and for that it was ideal for building and loading ships for commerce.

News of the landing of white men in present-day Wilmington took just a few days to travel up the Brandywine in the early seventeenth century. In barter for European merchandise, the Lenni-Lenape of the Delaware River Valley brought pelts from the winter hunt, mainly deer, as well as bear, red fox, and rabbit. The colony was centered on trade with the Indians for beaver skins, which were highly valued in Europe, and the Swedish government populated the colony with deported minor lawbreakers and soldiers who had deserted. Thus Sweden was the first to claim the land of what was then called Delaware County, Pennsylvania, and soon settled here with Dutch and Finnish colonists.

Along the Christina waterfront, upriver half a mile from its confluence with the Brandywine and the Delaware, a monument by Swedish sculptor Carl Milles commemorates the landing at the rocks. The Swedes had played an important role in the settling of this Middle-Atlantic region—they had opened the first liaison with the Indians, enabling the English to follow and continue settlement. The earliest settlers of New Sweden were the first to piece together the hewn notches of log cabins, packing them with sphagnum moss for a simple, sturdy construction that would carry westward with the expansion of the frontier in America. Swedes and Finns built the first mills, breweries, schools, and courts, and the first shipbuilding yards. Three centuries later, volunteer shipbuilders are bracing the wooden whale-sized ribs of a schooner. The boat will be a working replica of The Kalmar Nyckel, that Dutch-built flagship which set sail from Sweden in 1635. The original schooner is resting beneath the sea off the coast of Kalmar, yet just as the history of the first settlers to walk on the rocks of the Christina's shoal survives, the new ship—91 feet long on deck, 129 tons, with 12 guns—will help revive the enterprise that grew to a small empire on the Christina's waterfront.

The Swedes built Fort Christina in Wilmington, claimed the west shore of the Delaware River, and purchased the land from the Indians. It wasn't long before the Dutch grew hostile toward the Swedish leader Johan Printz' increasing control of the fur trade along the Delaware.

Dick Grant aboard "Go Go"

The Dutch government believed New Sweden was in Dutch territory. Peter Stuyvesant, the newly appointed governor of New Netherland, challenged New Sweden's governor by building a fort of his own in 1651—Fort Casimir on the shore at New Castle, five miles below, where the Delaware River becomes a bay. Printz returned to Sweden, and his successor, Johan Claudius Rising, led the Swedish settlers attack to capture the Dutch fort in 1654, and renamed it Fort "Trefalighet" or Trinity.

In retaliation, Dutch leader Peter Stuyvesant dispatched hundreds of men aboard seven ships. To regain control Stuyvesant destroyed Christinaham, the village outside Fort Christina, in 1655, ending the political rule of Sweden in the New World. The Swedes surrendered that September and their land became part of New Netherland.

There were 130 households in New Sweden at the time, and with prosperity, religious freedom, and opportunity in their native land, few Swedes or Finns wished to travel to America after that initial settlement. European wars and great distance drew Sweden's royal attention away from the New World.

Those circumstances opened the way for the English to take control of the Delaware River in 1664. England was then under James, Duke of York, who was granted the Delaware counties by royal charter of his brother King Charles II. The British had captured all of New Netherland, including the Brandywine, and ruled the settlements as part of the colony of New York. The Dutch would recapture the land once again in 1673, but turn it over peacefully to the English the next year.

William Penn wanted to establish an invulnerable route between his colony (that included Chester County) and the Atlantic Ocean. In 1682, England gave Penn the Delaware region as a territory of his Pennsylvania colony, and the Delaware region became known as the Three Lower Counties. All remaining Swedes, Finns, and Dutch fell under the rule of William Penn during the next several decades and Pennsylvania governors ruled the Delaware counties until the Revolutionary War. The Old Swedes Church, built of Brandywine stone and Swedish brick by the early settlers, has remained beside the Christina.

Nearby the Brandywine ends, in a sense, as it begins. Quietly. Just a few hundred yards from the constant, dim roar of Interstate 495 in

Pages 198,199: Tugs

Brandywine Tugboat

200

south Wilmington, the river widens to join the Christina estuary and edges toward the larger Delaware. When I-495 was built atop pilings through marshland to the west, the nesting grounds and habitat for several species of birds and animals were destroyed. Downriver, just a few hundred yards from a salvage yard where the souls of cars await reclamation, Dick Grant is puttering in his marina nestled into the crook of the Brandywine and the Christina.

Grant says the creek is diminishing with the silt and debris, carried down from the highlands and over the dams at Lenape and Hagley, that settles around the mouth of the river. "That's Chadds Ford Dirt," he says, pointing to a fresh, smooth earthen mound along the northern bank. "All the dirt from Pennsylvania piles up on our land." Like a bathtub, the Brandywine drains a large basin through one small opening, and while barges continue to dredge the Christina, the barely navigated Brandywine is left untouched. It is navigable through a twenty-foot channel, and Dick, with his tiny outboard, is one of the few to travel its path up toward the first dam.

He and his two dogs, Tattoo and Baby Girl, share a trailer that nestles between the boats—big old cruisers with names like Cloud Nine and Mariah. Grant knows he has his rotting boats plopped on a Realtor's gold mine. He sold the land a few years ago, but not the buildings, the business, or "Go Go," his 48-foot cruiser. They are his as long as he can breathe the marsh air.

"Yeah, I sold it, but I can live here as long as I'm alive. I figured I'd be better off taking the money, 'cause I don't have anybody to leave the place to," Grant says. Thirty-two years ago, when he opened the marina, the waterfront wasn't much different than it is now. But it will change. Dick knows it will change, the mayor knows, and particularly the developers, for already the plans are being drawn to develop the Christina riverfront with restaurants and stores north of Swedes Landing. Several plans have been drawn, some aspire to be a small Inner Harbor or a South Street Seaport.

"Up the Creek" is the small restaurant Grant built in the early seventies, a few hundred yards from the bridge that carries the superhighway over the estuary. When the dim bar fills at midday, Patsy Kline belts out "Crazy" on the jukebox. And on warm summer evenings, the back room along the docks is alive with dance and drink.

At the long tables, Grant serves muskrats trapped in the marshes to the east along the Delaware. "We fry 'em," he says. "Served with stewed tomatoes and peppers, muskrat taste like Chicken Cacciatore." Occasionally his trapper friend out west freezes enough of his take that Dick can add possum, coon, deer, bear, moose hot dogs, rattlesnake, frog legs, elk, and boar to his menu for his sellout Wild Game Dinners.

The pickup trucks in the gravel lot are far removed from the Amish buggies that crossed this river when it was nothing more than a trickle. Yet the laughter of the local people on the deck is familiar. It really is not so different from the Stolzfus family ice cream socials and the October wedding parties forty miles to the north. Here, where North turns into South and life begins to take on a drawl and twang, the laughter and the smiles are not all that different.

The river is even wider alongside Grant's boatyard than it appears. Great rusted barges extend the banks. At high tide they are flush with the land, camouflaged against the ground by loose hunks of brown, crumbling iron and steel. Cranes, cables, and great corroded chains weight the long, hulking cargo boats and make them stand solid as ground in the motionless water.

Just beyond are the tugs, this quiet stretch of water their graveyard. A pair of rusty boats lean against each other like beached horseshoe crabs in the gray water. Four other tugs have some life in their steel, but they are being stripped of hardware, and it is likely that they will never run the Delaware again. The one closest to shore, tied to the barge with two-inch lines, her bow facing the mouth of the ebbing river, is banded in the creamy yellow and brown paint of the other tugs. This one sports a name tag. Big white letters across a peeling wooden plank proclaim BRANDYWINE as the water slides past her hull.

Meanwhile, about forty miles north of Dick's marina, there's a small hole in the side of Welsh Mountain. And from that hole sprinkles the sweet water that will someday be here. The water will carry with it the Amish farmer's soil from the highland tributaries and Chadds Ford dirt, it will be taken up from the creek to follow the pipes that flow beneath the towns and city, it will flow through history and rebirth and will come to this spot as the water always does. And then, like its tributaries in the north, first grown from tiny springs, the Brandywine will give itself to larger water that meets the sea.

CHRONOLOGY

1525 – The Anabaptist movement, from which Amish and Mennonites descend, begins in Zurich, Switzerland.

1638 – Kalmar Nyckel carries first Swedish settlers to America to The Rocks near the mouth of the Brandywine. New Sweden is established in present-day Wilmington.

1654 – Swedes and Finns capture the Dutch Fort Casimir in New Castle.

1655 – The Dutch, under Peter Stuyvesant, capture the entire New Sweden colony, ending the political rule of Sweden in the New World.

1664 – The English, under James, Duke of York, control the Delaware River.

1681 – Pennsylvania Charter granted William Penn to settle debt with King Charles of England.

1682 – William Penn names Chester, Bucks and Philadelphia his three original colonies. English and Welsh Quakers venture to Philadelphia, and lands west. The northern Lenni-Lenapes see white man for the first time.
Jacob Vandever given permission to build a gristmill on land along the Brandywine in present-day Wilmington, agreeing to pay Penn or his heirs one-half bushel of wheat annually.

1683 – William Penn buys land from Indians.

1684 – Birmingham Township established.

1703 – Downingtown Log House built along the edge of the wilderness.

1705 – Delaware chiefs insist that they had been deeded land by Penn. Fight to regain a mile on each side of Brandywine from its mouth to the West Branch.

1706 – Penn's Commissioners of Property use Indian Rock, on the lower West Branch, to mark the southern boundary of Lenni-Lenape land that continues north to the source, one mile on either side of the creek.
Brinton's mill, one of the last to run flour on the Brandywine, is built.

1710 – First settlers arrive in Honey Brook.

1718 – Plans to build Birmingham Friends Meeting House are under way.

1729 – Scotch-Irish sail from Ulster to the American Colonies, arriving first in New Castle.

1737 – John Chads is advanced money by the Chester County Commissioners to enable him to build a boat and establish a ferry aross the Brandywine.

1739 – King George II grants charter whereby people of "Willington" can form self-governing borough and hold markets. Name is changed to Wilmington at the king's request.

1740 – Indians leave Springton Manor.
First water-powered sawmill on the upper Brandywine near Beaver Dam.

1741 – Thomas Canby comes to Wilmington with sons Thomas, Jr. and Oliver.

1742 – Oliver Canby builds first merchant mill on the Brandywine.

1744 – Committee meets with Governor Thomas to settle feud over Scots on Springton Manor. Some "squatters" vacate to the Susquehanna Valley or Virginia.

1767 – Mason-Dixon line established.

1773 – Humphry Marshall cultivates botanical gardens of forest and ornamental plants.

1777 – Battle of the Brandywine fought: a victory for the British.

1787 – Joshua and Thomas Gilpin establish paper mill below Rockford Mills.

1789 – Delaware County is created after breaking apart from Chester County.

1795 – Delawarean Jacob Broom establishes first cotton factory in the U.S., on the Brandywine at Rising Sun.

1796 – Public works system initiated for Wilmington.

1799 – Federal Slitting Mill of the Rokeby Iron Works established.

1802 – Indian Hannah dies, estimated 71 years of age.
E. I. du Pont builds powder mills along the Brandywine.

1803 – The stately home of E. I. du Pont is built: Eleutherian Mills.

1807 – Marshall's-Northbrook Bridge erected, the first covered bridge in Chester County.

1810 – Isaac Pennock establishes Brandywine Iron Works and Nail Factory in Coatesville: the predecessor to Lukens Steel.

1811 – Cambridge, at the head of the West Branch, laid out in lots by means of a lottery.
E. I. du Pont's brother Victor sets up residence and textile mill on east bank across from the mills.

1812 – The War of 1812 launches the success of the du Pont mills with its call for gun powder.

1813 – Rebecca Pennock, daughter of the iron master, marries Philadelphia physician Charles Lloyd Lukens, who enters iron trade with father-in-law.

1814 – The Henry Clay Mill is constructed as a cotton spinning mill downstream from the Hagley powder works.

1816 – Joshua and Thomas Gilpin obtain patent for first continuous roll paper manufacturing machine in U.S.
Charles Lloyd Lukens takes over operations at Coatesville iron mill.

1825 – Fire destroys the Gilpin paper mills in Wilmington.
Rebecca Lukens, widowed, takes over her husband's iron works in Coatesville.
An elderly Lafayette travels to the Brandywine battleground, pointing out to the crowds gathered there the spot where he was wounded. He returns to France aboard the frigate Brandywine, placed at his disposal by Congress.

1826 – Stone arch bridge carries Strasburg Road across creek at Mortonville.

1827 – Wilmington begins drawing water from the Brandywine.

1831 – Coatesville becomes first stop on the Wilmington & Northern Line.
Joseph Bancroft begins the manufacture of cotton cloth at Rockford.

1834 – A bridge is built over the Brandywine at Seed's Ford (present-day Wawaset) and the name of the town is changed to Seed's Bridge.

1837 – Iron master Charles Brooke begins business with two forges, rolling mill, grist and saw mills at Hibernia.

1839 – A January flood raises Brandywine 22 feet, destroying mills and bridges.

1840 – First turbine comes to the Brandywine after papermaker Gilpin witnesses one while on a trip to France.

1845 – James Riddle establishes Kentmere Mills for processing cotton in the former Gilpin paper building.

1852 – Wallace Township founded.

1857 – Financial panic precipitated by the closing of the Ohio Life and Trust Companies impacts Brandywine merchants and millers.

1859 – Philadelphia and Baltimore Central completed through Chadds Ford *en route* to Oxford.

1861 – Downingtown & Waynesburg Railroad opened to traffic.

1865 – Surveys for the Wilmington and Reading Railroad begin.
Joseph Bancroft admits sons William Poole and Samuel Bancroft, Jr. into a partnership known as Joseph Bancroft & Sons.
1868 – Meeting held to discuss public park along the Brandywine in Wilmington. City Council moves to purchase land. Injunction obtained by taxpayers who object to expense.
1869 – First section of Wilmington & Reading Railroad on West Branch completed.
1873 – Financial panic brings downfall of the Wilmington & Reading Railroad.
1874 – Joseph Bancroft dies at Rockford of pneumonia in his 72nd year.
Iron Bridge spans the river between Eleutherian Mills and Louviers.
1876 – Wilmington & Reading Railroad sold; reorganized the following year as the Wilmington & Northern.
1883 – Plans for a Brandywine Park in Wilmington (abandoned in 1868 because of public dissent) resume with the appointment of a Park Commission.
1884 – The Du Pont Company converts the Henry Clay mill from the manufacture of textiles to the production of powder containers.
1889 – Brandywine Granite Co. formed above Wilmington. Quarried stone that supplied the Delaware Breakwater and other government projects.
1889 – Joseph Bancroft & Sons Co. incorporated.
1893 – Washington Memorial Bridge spans the lower Brandywine at a cost of $79,000. The residential Washington Heights grows as a result.
Brandywine Club established, for the "social intercourse and amusement" of Du Pont employees and their families.
1894 – Brandywine amusement park near Lenape pulls in 3500 daytrippers on a summer day, reportedly because of the sponsorship of a Reading brewery offering free beer to all.
1895 – Brandywine Park Station closed.
Colonel Swayne buys Hibernia property and adds wings for servants' quarters to his new mansion.
1898 – Howard Pyle sets up studio and Brandywine School in Chadds Ford grist mill.
1901 – William Poole Bancroft organizes the Woodlawn Trust to carry out land preservation and development plans beyond his lifetime.
1902 – N. C. Wyeth begins studies with Howard Pyle.
1904 – Bancroft begins his 19-year term as president of the Wilmington Board of Park Commissioners.
1906 – Chris Sanderson and his mother rent half of Washington's headquarters.
1907 – Du Pont moves offices from the Brandywine to downtown Wilmington.
1922 – Washington Memorial Bridge replaced with current structure.
1925 – Brandywine Creek bridge at 14th Street, lower Wilmington, is built of lattice iron.
1928 – North Market Street Bridge built beside Wilmington waterworks, the sixth on the site since the first wooden one in the 1760s.
1929 – Last trolley runs to the Brandywine Park from West Chester.
1931 – Sanforizing machine installed at Bancroft Mills.
1933 – Hoopes reservoir is formed beside Red Clay Creek, augmenting the water supplied by the Brandywine for the City of Wilmington.
Last water-powered mill alongside Rockland Dam closes.
1934 – First organized meeting of the Amphibious Order of Frogs, Downingtown.
1937 – The wooden Painter's Bridge that spanned the creek at Rt. 926, Pocopson, is replaced with concrete.

1939 – Bancroft Mills produces "Everglaze" – a durable chintz for drapery and upholstery.

1942 – A flood on the West Brandywine damages dams, mills, properties. Influences decision to strictly enforce encroachment onto the flood plain.

1945 – The Brandywine Valley Authority, America's first watershed protection organization, is founded.
Brinton's Mill stops operating.

1948 – Spring blizzard takes area farmers by surprise.

1949 – Pennsylvania Historical and Museum Commission purchases land in Chadds Ford to form Brandywine Battlefield State Park.

1958 – Andrew Wyeth buys old Brinton's Mill.

1963 – County of Chester purchases a private estate on the West Branch, for use as a county park. Cost of Hibernia: $130,000 for 700 acres.

1964 – Brandywine Creek State Park is formed, the first state park built with federal matching land and water conservation funds.

1966 – Brandywine Creek State Park nature center is built.

1967 – The Brandywine Conservancy founded to address land and water conservation and land development.

1969 – State fish and game department installs fish ladders at dams along the creek in Wilmington.

1971 – The Brandywine River Museum opens.

1972 – Hurricane Agnes damages property along the creek.

1980 – Amish barnraisings begin on LeBoutellier Tract in Honey Brook.

1981 – Horatio E. Myrick bequeaths his 212-acre farm, house and historic barn to the Brandywine Valley Association.
Purchase donation from Woodlawn Trust adds 350 acres to Brandywine Creek State Park.

1988 – Wilmington celebrates its 350th year since settlement by the Swedes.
Chester County Parks and Recreation opens Springton Manor Farm.
The lower Brandywine is designated a Scenic River by the Pennsylvania Department of Environmental Resources.

BIBLIOGRAPHY

Bounds, Harvey, *Bancroft Mills 1831-1961. One Hundred Thirty Years of Fine Textile Products*, Wilmington, 1961.

Canby, Henry Seidel, *The Brandywine*, The Rivers of America, 1941.

Davis, A.M., *Among the Willows*, Appleton's Journal No. 118, Vol. VI July 1, 1871.

Department of Environmental Resources and the Brandywine Conservancy, *Lower Brandywine Scenic Rivers Evaluation and Management Study*, 1987.

Eppihimer, Margaret, *Headwaters of the Brandywine... A History of Honey Brook Township*, Honey Brook Township Board of Supervisors, 1983.

Godfrey, Michael A., *A Sierra Club Naturalist's Guide to the Piedmont*, Sierra Club Books, 1980.

Hagley Foundation, Inc., *The Hagley Museum Guide, Eleutherian Mills*, 1976.

Hoffecker, Carol E., *Brandywine Village: The Story of a Milling Community*, Old Brandywine Village, Inc., Wilmington, 1974.

Heathcote, Charles William, *History of Chester County*. Horace F. Temple, West Chester, 1926.

James, Arthur E., *Covered Bridges of Chester County, Pennsylvania*, The Chester County Historical Society, West Chester, 1976.

James, Arthur E., *A History of Birmingham Township*, Chester County Historical Society, West Chester, 1971.

Laird, William Winder, *The Iron Bridge Over the Brandywine 1874-1974*, The Cedar Tree Press, Inc., 1974.

MacElree, Wilmer W., *Along the Western Brandywine*, printed by F. S. Hickman, West Chester, 1912.

New Castle County Department of Planning, *The Brandywine Valley Scenic River and Highway Study*, 1987.

Sanderson, Christian C., *A Bit of Rhyme . . . Back East on the Brandywine*, Chadds Ford, reprinted 1965.

Umbarger, Mary, *Who Owns the Brandywine?*, The Land, Vol VII, No. 3, Baltimore, 1948.

University of Penn., Institute for Environmental Studies, *The Plan and Program For the Brandywine*, Philadelphia, 1968.

Wallace Twp. Historical Commission, *Wallace Township: Born of Controversy in 1852*, 1977.

Weslager, C.A., *Red Men on the Brandywine*, Hambleton Company, Inc., Wilmington, 1953.

West Brandywine Township, *Between the Brandywines. . . 300 Years of Heritage*, 1984.

Wilmington Board of Health, *Impurities in the Brandywine River: Report of the Special Committee of the Board of Health of the City of Wilmington*, Wilmington, 1873.

Wilmington, City of: Department of Public Works, *Wilmington Water Supply*, Wilmington, 1979.

Zebley, Frank, *Along the Brandywine*, Wilmington, 1940.

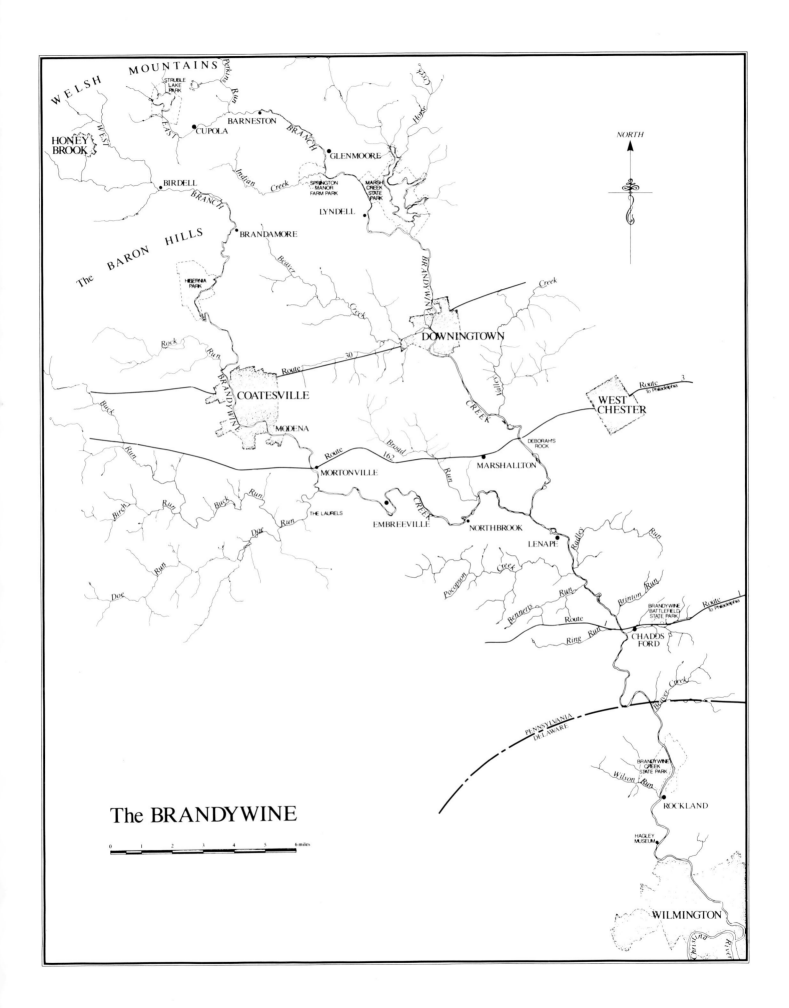

The BRANDYWINE

WELSH MOUNTAINS

HONEY BROOK

STRUBLE LAKE PARK

CUPOLA

BARNESTON

GLENMOORE

BIRDELL

Perkins Run

Indian Creek

Hoske Creek

BRANCH

SPRINGTON MANOR FARM PARK

MARSH CREEK STATE PARK

LYNDELL

BRANDAMORE

Beaver Creek

THE BARON HILLS

HIBERNIA PARK

Rock Run

Route 30

BRANDYWINE

DOWNINGTOWN

Creek

NORTH

COATESVILLE

Buck Run

MODENA

Route 162

Broad Run

Valley CREEK

WEST CHESTER

Route 3 To Philadelphia

DEBORAH'S ROCK

MORTONVILLE

MARSHALLTON

Birch Run

Buck Run

THE LAURELS

CREEK

Doe Run

EMBREEVILLE

NORTHBROOK

LENAPE

Radley Run

Run

Pocopson Creek

Bennetts Run

Run

Brinton Run

BRANDYWINE BATTLEFIELD STATE PARK

Route 1 To Philadelphia

Route 1

Ring Run

CHADDS FORD

PENNSYLVANIA
DELAWARE

Beaver Creek

BRANDYWINE CREEK STATE PARK

Wilson Run

ROCKLAND

HAGLEY MUSEUM

WILMINGTON

Christiana River

0 1 2 3 4 5 6 miles

209

PHOTO INDEX

210

ABOUT THE AUTHOR

ELIZABETH HUMPHREY began her writing career as a staff reporter for the *Daily Local News* (Chester County). Her articles on travel and the arts have appeared in *County Lines Magazine, Historic Preservation, Mid-Atlantic Country, The Philadelphia Inquirer* and the *Wilmington News Journal.* A graduate of Western Connecticut State University, she studied writing in London and at Harvard University. She lives in West Chester, Pennsylvania.

ABOUT THE PHOTOGRAPHER

MICHAEL KAHN's sensitive portraits of the Brandywine and its people combine his love of the outdoors and concern for the preservation of the Brandywine Valley's landscape. A lifelong resident of Chester County, Pennsylvania, Michael works as a commercial photographer and has contributed to several regional and national publications and exhibitions.